THE NORMANS

for my mother

THE NORMANS

Trevor Rowley

TEMPUS

First published 1999

PUBLISHED IN THE UNITED KINGDOM BY:

Tempus Publishing Ltd
The Mill, Brimscombe Port
Stroud, Gloucestershire GL5 2QG

PUBLISHED IN THE UNITED STATES OF AMERICA BY:

Tempus Publishing Inc.
2A Cumberland Street
Charleston, SC 29401

Tempus books are available in France, Germany and Belgium
from the following addresses:

Tempus Publishing Group	Tempus Publishing Group	Tempus Publishing Group
21 Avenue de la République	Gustav-Adolf-Straße 3	Place de L'Alma 4/5
37300 Joué-lès-Tours	99084 Erfurt	1200 Brussels
FRANCE	GERMANY	BELGIUM

British Library Cataloguing in Publication Data.
A catalogue record for this book is available from the British Library.

ISBN 0 7524 1434 8

Typesetting and origination by Tempus Publishing.
PRINTED AND BOUND IN GREAT BRITAIN.

Contents

Illustrations

Colour illustrations

Acknowledgements

Thanks are due to all those who have helped in the creation of this book: to Peter Kemmis Betty for encouraging me to write it and for providing the opportunity to travel in France and in Italy; to Esther Paist for help with the section on Norman music and to colleagues both in Oxford and elsewhere who have talked with me about various aspects of the Norman world; to Liz Miller and Sheila Lester for producing the typescript and to Mélanie Steiner for the plans.

The cover photograph shows Byzantine followers of Robert Guiscard, Duke of Apulia.

Introduction

In the English-speaking world, the Normans are almost always thought of in the context of William the Conqueror and his defeat of Harold of England at the Battle of Hastings in 1066. The processes by which Normandy came into being and the activities of Normans in other parts of Europe, notably southern Italy and the Levant, are little known except by Norman enthusiasts and specialist scholars. It is the aim of this book to bring the story of the Norman achievement to the general reader — not only the Normans in Normandy and England, but also their activities in the Mediterranean — and to assess the overall place of the Normans in medieval history and their impact in its entirety.

The Norman story at first seems deceptively straightforward: the area which was to become known as Normandy was ceded to the Vikings by the western Carolingian empire in the early tenth century and then went on to develop as the most powerful principality in northern France. The energy, ruthlessness and administrative ability of the Normans enabled them to subdue and, in some cases, annex their Frankish neighbours and also to mount a military campaign that was able to defeat a formidable united Anglo-Saxon kingdom in England. In addition, Normans were able to conquer the Byzantines and Latins in southern Italy and the Moslems in Sicily, thereby creating a powerful Mediterranean kingdom consisting of southern Italy and Sicily known as the 'Two Sicilies'. This kingdom provided the springboard for the conquest of Malta and a large section of the North African coast. Normans, from both north-western Europe and Italy, were involved in the First Crusade, enabling them to establish a formidable presence in the Holy Land and a crusader kingdom at Antioch in the Levant. Norman armies, sometimes by themselves and sometimes with allies, also undertook campaigns in Spain, the Balkans and the Aegean and were even capable of besieging Constantinople at the heart of the Byzantine Empire. The scale of the Norman achievement has prompted some scholars to talk of an interrupted Norman empire stretching from Wales in the west to Syria in the east and from Scotland in the north to Tunis in the south (**1**).

Such, then, are the bare bones of the Norman story between AD 900 and 1200, yet each of these above statements masks numerous questions and caveats which need to be addressed if we are to understand more fully the character and nature of the Norman world. The term 'Norman' is simply French for 'Scandinavian', and was applied to the inhabitants of the region of France taken over by Vikings in the tenth century — the *Terra Northmannorum* or the *Northmannia*. The general perception is that the Normans who came to conquer England with William were essentially Vikings who had been converted to Christianity. There is, however, considerable evidence to suggest that by the beginning of the eleventh century Normandy was essentially a Frankish principality, in many respects not unlike its neighbours. There are also serious questions to be asked about the Viking character of early Normandy, particularly about the numbers of Scandinavians who

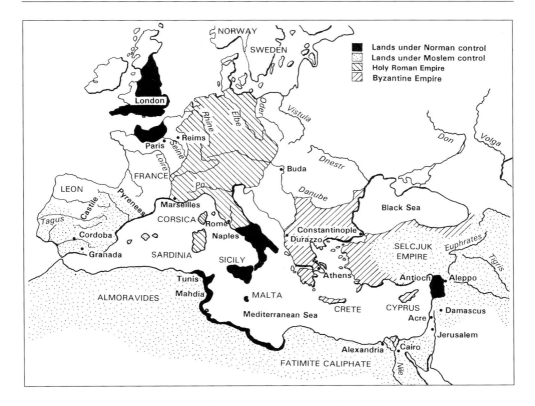

1   Map showing the full extent of Norman possessions in the twelfth century

migrated and colonised the duchy. It now appears that a relatively small number of Scandinavians took over the reins of power in the tenth century from the Franks and, although there was limited later migration by Viking settlers into Normandy, it was on nowhere near the scale imagined by earlier historians. By the middle of the eleventh century there is little evidence of Viking culture surviving in Normandy and, although William himself was directly descended from a Viking war-lord (Rollo), few of the knights and their followers that defeated the English at Hastings had Viking blood in their veins. The Franks for the most part had assimilated the Vikings and the resulting cultural blend was Norman.

Nevertheless, it is an indisputable fact that in 1066 William, Duke of Normandy, defeated and killed King Harold of England at the battle of Hastings and went on to take the English throne. There is, however, room for doubt about the long-term impact of the Conquest of England. The immediate impact of the Norman take-over of Anglo-Saxon England was dramatic and at times brutal. The military conquest was associated with a total transfer of land ownership from Anglo-Saxon thegns to continental knights. The Domesday Book (1086) provides a vivid account, within its sombre and painstaking record, of the way in which England passed from Anglo-Saxon ownership to Norman hands. At face value the Domesday Book indicates a peaceful and well-organised transfer of land from Saxon to Norman; but on the ground the story must have been very different, with much local violence, suffering and confusion. By 1086, out of 10,000 holdings only a handful remained in Saxon hands. It was probably true that Saxons often continued as manorial reeves, and perhaps were often able to maintain a considerable degree of control, but the political and military reality was that the Normans had won, and that they took all the spoils. Similarly in the Church, Saxon leaders were comprehensively replaced by Normans and their allies. Nevertheless at grass roots level there was even less Norman folk settlement in England than there had been Scandinavian settlement in Normandy. Furthermore, the families of those Normans that did come to England with William were rapidly anglicised, and within a century of the Conquest it is far more accurate to refer to Anglo-Norman England than to Norman England.

Even at this distance of time it is difficult for the English to view the Normans objectively. English attitudes to the Norman Conquest display a persistent mixture of fascination, admiration and incredulity. Fascination with the very fact of the last continental conquest of England, admiration towards those that undertook the venture, and incredulity that the forces of this small duchy could overcome the English who were fighting on home soil.

Attitudes to the Norman Conquest of England and to their subsequent occupation have fluctuated considerably over the last centuries. The concept of the 'Norman yoke' has been part of popular English mythology over the generations. Sir Henry Spellman (d.1641) and Sir Robert Cotton (d.1631) traced many illegal abuses back to the Normans and the Norman feudal system, a theme enthusiastically taken up and developed by nineteenth-century writers such as Charles Kingsley and George Burrow. The perception was that before 1066 the Anglo-Saxons lived as free and equal citizens, governed by representative institutions. It was thought that the Norman Conquest was responsible for depriving the English of these liberties, establishing the tyranny of an alien king and alien landlords. Theories of this nature were almost certainly in vogue throughout the Middle Ages and account for the popularity of Edward the Confessor, both as an English king and saint, and King Alfred, who assumed the role of symbol of national independence. Thomas Paine (1737–1809) went one stage further and attributed all the problems that England experienced after 1066 to 'the French bastard and his banditti.'

During the Victorian period there was a tendency to regard the Norman Conquest in a more positive light and as marking the start of the present line of monarchy. By the 1930s, historical attitudes had changed once more and scholars such as Sayles suggested that the Norman Conquest was only a minor irritation that did little to interrupt the continuum of Anglo-Saxon society and institutions. This attitude hardened during the Second World War in the face of another continental threat to the British Isles and some scholars, such as Sir Frank Stenton, who had previously seen the Norman Conquest as a watershed, came down on the side of continuity. In recent years the divide has tended to concentrate on differences between archaeologists and historians. Medieval archaeologists, with concepts of cultural continuity, have found it difficult to accept that the Conquest affected all but a relatively small section of society. While some historians, such as Allen Brown, have emphasised the Norman achievement on a European scale, others have been more circumspect and pointed to the essentially adaptable nature of Norman society that in England was the blend of Anglo-Saxon and Norman, and in Italy a mixture Norman, Moslem and Byzantine. In recent years scholars have used the phrase 'aristocratic diaspora' to describe European events in the tenth to thirteenth centuries during the course of which lords and knights from the heartlands of the former Carolingian empire conquered and settled lands — England, Spain, Italy, Greece — on the periphery of Latin Christendom.

Although much of the evidence for the Norman Conquest of England is historical in character, there is enough physical evidence to provide the archaeologist with a unique opportunity of examining an invasion of Britain within the context of a wealth of documentary evidence. It is generally accepted that the Norman Conquest of England was achieved by a relatively small force, in total no more than 10,000 people, and, although there was some migration from continental Europe into England following the Conquest, there was no major population movement. In some areas, such as warfare and the church, there were fundamental changes, whereas in others, such as rural settlement (apart from in the north of England where many post-Conquest villages appear to have been founded), the impact of the Conquest was imperceptible.

What of the Normans in southern Europe? The Norman take-over in Italy was very different from the Conquest of England. It was led by groups of Norman mercenary soldiers, fighting largely for Byzantine princes in the first instance. It was also a protracted affair, lasting for more than a century before Roger was proclaimed first King of Sicily. Almost every political and cultural aspect of Norman Sicily was different from that of the Norman territories in north-western Europe. Whereas the Normans in England became anglicised, the Normans in Italy took on characteristics of Latin, Byzantine and even Moslem society. There were relatively few Norman settlers in southern Europe, although the Norman Conquest heralded the replacement of Sicilian Moslems by Latin settlers. The Norman achievement in Italy was to bring southern Italy back into the western European orbit after centuries of Byzantine and Moslem control.

The Normans were an extraordinarily eclectic group of people who adopted and adapted the customs of the peoples they conquered with the result that Norman societies in different parts of the world were widely varied. Indeed, the capacity of the Normans to adopt the cultural characteristics of those peoples they conquered prompted one historian to question whether they had a distinct identity at all (see R.H.C. Davis *The Normans and Their Myth*). It is perhaps best to view the Normans as a catalytic people who changed the societies they came in contact with by their presence rather than by culturally dominating them.

Although the Norman impact on the medieval world was significant, political Norman societies were everywhere relatively short-lived. In England, strictly speaking, the Norman dynasty came to an end with the death of King Stephen in 1154. Normandy itself was eclipsed as an independent duchy in 1204, when the French king defeated the forces of King John of England and absorbed it into French territory. The Norman Kingdom of the Two Sicilies came to an end by the end of the twelfth century when the German Hohenstaufens replaced the line of the Norman Tancredis. The Norman occupation of the North African littoral lasted for less than 20 years, while the longest surviving of Norman territories was perhaps the least Norman in nature, that at Antioch in what is now Turkey and Syria, which did not finally fall until 1268. Yet despite the short time-span of Norman ascendancy, it is clear that the Normans were responsible for considerable political and cultural achievements and that without them the medieval world may have been significantly different.

1 Vikings, Norsemen and Normans — the making of Normandy

The Duchy of Normandy emerged in the tenth century out of the region known in the post Roman era as the Breton or Neustrian March, an area which occupied the western edge of the decaying Frankish or Carolingian Empire. Neustria meant 'New West Land' in contrast to Austrasia (East Land). It was the inhabitants of Neustria who first used the term 'Francia' for the Western Kingdom of the Carolingian Empire. 'Frank' was derived from the old Germanic word for members of the tribe on the Rhine which conquered the country that became France. According to the rather scanty surviving historical records, the legal origins of Normandy date from 911 when a Scandinavian war-lord called Rollo, or Hrólfr, was created Count of Rouen and granted the lower Seine valley by Charles the Simple, king of the western Franks. Before this, there had been Viking activity in north-western France for at least the previous half century, during which time towns, villages and monasteries were plundered in just the same way as eastern and central England was being regularly attacked on the other side of the English Channel. Evidence of Viking settlement in Normandy during this early phase has been difficult to identify, but it seems likely that there had already been some Scandinavian colonisation in the region before 900. The Franks used the word 'Normand' to describe the Viking peoples and this word soon came to be synonymous with the region taken over by Rollo and his Scandinavian followers.

The Carolingian Empire

The Carolingian Empire had extended over much of modern France and Germany and had reached its greatest extent under the Emperor Charlemagne, after whom it was named. Its capital was at Aix-la-Chapelle (Aachen) in Westphalia (2). The Carolingian Empire inherited many of the administrative structures of the Roman Empire on which it was loosely based, but it extended far to the east of the Rhine, the conventional northern European frontier of the Roman world. In the late eighth century, the Carolingian Empire appeared to be about to reconstitute the pan-European empire of the Romans, particularly after Charlemagne was crowned Emperor of the Romans by Pope Leo III on Christmas Day 800. This event effectively marked the beginning of that curious but persistent medieval phenomenon, the Holy Roman Empire, which continued to mould together the fragmented Germanic world throughout the Middle Ages (3).

Charlemagne was an imperialist who extended his military activity into Saxony, into Moslem Spain where he created the Spanish March, into northern Italy and into central Eastern Europe. The Franks were anxious to claim for themselves what they could of the Roman legacy and this meant bringing architectural styles to Aix from Ravenna, where the late Roman imperial court had left a more dramatic architectural and artistic legacy than

2   *The palace chapel at Aix-la-Chapelle (Aachen) (ninth century). Capital of Charlemagne's empire*

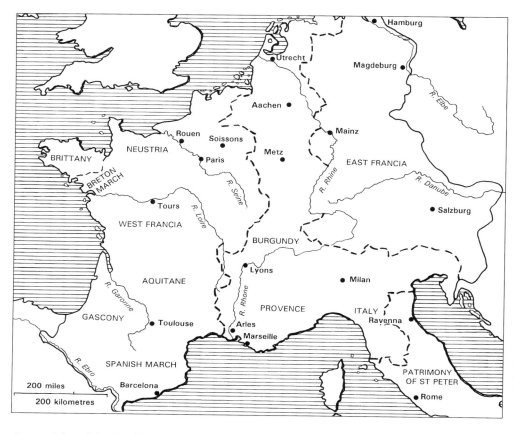

3   Map of the Carolingian Empire

Rome itself. The Carolingian Empire, however, did not have time to take root before it began to fall apart. The governance of such a vast and complex empire proved cumbersome and only partly effective, yet there were strong elements within it which were to serve as models for many of the medieval successor Christian kingdoms of the west. Essentially, however, the empire lacked the military base of its Roman predecessor and proved to be too large for its rural manorial base, and following Charlemagne's death in 814 began the long, familiar process of disintegration, the inevitable fate of all empires in the fullness of time.

The Carolingian Empire was made up of a patchwork of principalities under the control of counts, viscounts and dukes. Initially these were closely tied to the Emperor and held their power directly from him. In the early stages there were few hereditary dynasties within the Empire, but by the middle of the ninth century the extended empire proved too cumbersome to be managed from a single centre and was again divided into three; in effect, Germany, France and the Middle Kingdom (Lorraine, Burgundy and Lombardy). These constituent principalities became increasingly powerful and they themselves evolved into semi-autonomous separate sub-kingdoms. Principalities such as Burgundy,

Aquitaine and Septimania (Toulouse), while still acknowledging the Emperor's sovereignty, were able to operate with an ever-increasing degree of independence. These sub-kingdoms were ruled over by dukes (*duces*) and princes (*principes*). In the tenth century, the great duchies began to fragment into their constituent counties. In the north of France, in addition to Normandy, Brittany, Anjou, Maine, Blois and Flanders all became important principalities under the control of counts. The royal lands, which were, effectively, the residue of the Carolingian Empire, contracted to the area around Paris and Orléans.

In addition to this internal fragmentation, the successors to the Carolingian Empire faced external threats from the Scandinavians in the north and west, the Bretons in the west and, to a lesser extent, from the Moslems in the south. After establishing a bridgehead in Spain in the early eighth century, Moslem forces rapidly took over most of the Iberian peninsula and moved north of the Pyrenees into Francia where their advance was eventually stopped at Poitiers by Charles Martel in 732. Subsequently, the Moslems withdrew from the north-west of the Iberian peninsula and from the area immediately to the south of the Pyrenees to consolidate their activities in the rest of Spain. Nevertheless, although the Moslem hold on mainland European territories was on the decline, partly as a result of their own civil wars, they were still extremely active in the Mediterranean and retained control of all the major island groups, including Sicily, which provided them with a base to attack and settle in the relatively weak Byzantine-controlled areas of southern Italy. They were also able to establish a foothold at Fraxinetum, which was not finally extinguished until 973.

The Vikings

To the north were the Scandinavians or the Vikings who, during the first Viking Age, put an indelible imprint on the political and demographic geography of Western Europe, most notably by the establishment of the Danelaw in north-eastern England and the creation of Normandy in the north-west of France. The Vikings have been traditionally portrayed as pirates; merciless barbarians who plundered and burned their way through Western Europe, intent on destruction and pillage. This deep-rooted popular prejudice about the Vikings can be traced back directly to contemporary ecclesiastical chroniclers who, because they were the custodians of much portable wealth, were frequently the first victims of Viking raids. It could, however, be argued that the Vikings simply represented an unwelcome new player in a crowded political world which had already demonstrated a considerable degree of ruthless violence, particularly against pagans (**4**). Charlemagne himself had laid Saxony to waste in order to convert it to Christianity, and similar examples of comprehensive premeditated ferocity are common to the whole Norman story.

The Vikings in Britain

The riches of churches and monasteries were obvious and easy pickings for the seaborne early pagan Vikings. In 793 the island monastery of Lindisfarne, off the Northumbrian coast, was plundered. On hearing of this attack, Alcuin (d.804), the Northumbrian monk-scholar then working at the palace school at Aix which he had founded for Charlemagne, wrote expressing his horror at the event: 'it is nearly 350 years that we and our fathers have

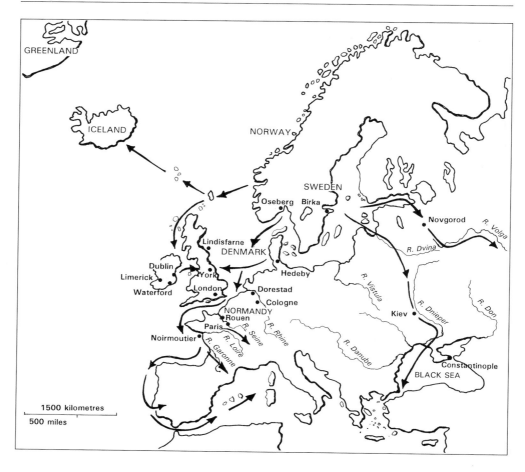

4   *Map showing Viking invasion routes in Western Europe. In the western Atlantic and the Mediterranean*

inhabited this most lovely land, and never before has such a terror appeared in Britain as we have now suffered from a pagan race, nor was it thought that such an inroad from the sea could be made'. He went on to imply that Charlemagne might secure by ransom the return of 'boys', i.e. noble children offered by their parents to the monastery, who had been carried off to Denmark. In 794 another Northumbrian monastery, probably Jarrow, was looted, and in 795 Iona was attacked. The first raid in Ireland was reported near Dublin in 795, and by 799 the raiders had reached as far south as the mainland European coast of Aquitaine. Although Scandinavian invaders and settlers had been involved in Western Europe on a modest scale from the fifth century onwards, the 'Viking Age' proper started in the last decade of the eighth century.

Settlement as well as plunder often followed acquisition of land; in this way Greenland, Iceland and the Scottish Islands were colonised in the second half of the ninth century. Yet when the Vikings arrived, these were largely empty lands where there was little opposition to their settlements. It was a very different story when their activity was directed against the politically sophisticated and culturally settled lands of Western Europe (**colour plate 1**).

In the first instance, the Vikings' over-riding interest was in portable wealth, usually precious metals, and this made churches and towns particularly vulnerable since the former were frequently used as treasuries for the regions surrounding them. Inevitably, this meant that initial Viking visits to England and later Normandy were characterised by violence. Within years such raids were replaced by a form of 'protection-racket' throughout western Europe, with a tax called the *Danegeld* being levied on Christian kingdoms in order to buy off the Scandinavians. Frankish and English rulers made *ad hoc* payments in the ninth century, but the whole process became more systematic in England after the defeat of the English at Maldon in Essex in 991. Enormous sums of money were raised and paid to the Danes during the latter half of the reign of King Æthelred, and the system of levying *geld* was refined and made more efficient under pressure of the need to meet escalating Danish demands. The use of *geld* to provide Viking fleets and trained elements in the army led to ambiguity in the use of the word, but the term *Danegeld* persisted in general use in England until the middle of the twelfth century.

Some scholars point out the more positive aspects of Viking activity; they came in relatively small numbers to begin with and the later phases of Viking incursion were associated with peaceful settlement. The results of the excavations of Viking York (*Jorvik*), for example, are often used to demonstrate a thriving and industrious, peaceful urban community, with trading links throughout Western Europe. It is certainly true that by the eleventh century the Scandinavians were operating in much more conventional political and military ways than their predecessors, but the Viking reputation for brutality was more difficult to transform.

In 851 a Viking army made the first attempt to winter in England, in Kent. Some 14 years later, in 865, the 'Great Army' landed in eastern England, when a Danish force came with the deliberate purpose of territorial conquest. The ancient kingdoms of Northumbria and Mercia were quickly conquered and a Viking territory was established in northern England, which eventually developed into the kingdom of York. Soon, East Anglia and most of Northumbria were under Danish rule, and Mercia was divided between the Saxons and the Danes. Effectively, only the southern kingdom of Wessex remained English. The whole of England might well have been overrun by the Vikings but for the determined defence of Alfred the Great of Wessex (871–99). Alfred defeated the Vikings at Edington (Somerset) (878), and the resulting political accommodation with Guthrum led to the departure of a large Viking force to northern Francia, allowing Alfred to undertake an ambitious defensive strategy which resulted in Wessex annexing areas of Mercia, including London.

Alfred and subsequent Saxon monarchs devised and developed a defensive system against the Vikings, firstly in the form of a navy and secondly with a series of fortified river crossing towns known as *burhs*. Some of these fortifications were newly erected at places such as Wallingford (Oxon) (**5**) and Wareham (Dorset), while others at centres such as Bath and Winchester re-used existing Roman defences. In fact, the ninth-century *burhs* represented the first systematic campaign of communal defence construction since Roman times. In England, the network of fortified towns created by Alfred and his successors helped revitalise urban life by providing safe locations for the transaction of

5   *Aerial view of the Saxon* burh *at Wallingford, Oxon*

trade and commerce. By 886 Alfred had made peace with Guthrum, and Alfred's son Edward the Elder had conquered all the Danish-held lands south of the river Humber. Saxon victories in England marked a crucial turning point in the history of the Vikings' relations with western Europe since, for the first time, a serious check had been imposed on their activities. The Vikings became aware that there were limits to what could be achieved by their traditional raiding activities in England. The military resistance in England resulted in the diversion of those Vikings who wished to continue raiding across the Channel into western Europe, thereby intensifying the pressure on the lands remaining under the control of the Frankish kings.

Alfred's success opened the way for a series of attempts to integrate the Vikings into western European life. The Treaty of Wedmore, agreed with Guthrum in 878, had sought a *modus vivendi* with the Vikings on the basis that he and his followers would, in return for their territory, keep the peace and convert to Christianity. This was a pattern of compromise frequently adopted to contain Viking forces, particularly in Francia. There were, indeed, significant advantages in this type of agreement for beleaguered native rulers, because, in theory at least, the Vikings' appetite for land was met, but confined within defined territorial limits. Also, the Viking poacher was obliged to turn gamekeeper by being given responsibility for maintaining order in the conquered lands; it was thus hoped to tame the Vikings by integrating them into the existing governmental and religious establishment.

The Vikings and the Carolingian Empire

In the second half of the ninth century the Vikings turned their attention to the great river estuaries of mainland Western Europe, in particular the Rhine, the Somme, the Seine and the Loire, which allowed access into the very heart of western mainland Europe. Even before Charlemagne's death, Viking raids along the North Sea coasts had presented the empire with formidable problems, and despite the revival of Frankish military strength epitomised by the growth in the strength of their cavalry, the Empire was ill-equipped to deal with maritime enemies. The first Viking ships arrived off the coast of France c.820, and by the middle of the ninth century Scandinavian incursions into France had become an annual occurrence. As early as Easter Sunday 845, the Viking leader, Ragnar, is said to have moved up the Seine to attack Paris. It is reputed that the emperor Charles II, 'The Bald', paid him 7000 pounds of silver to leave peacefully and to take his plunder with him (**colour plate 2**).

Specific involvement in the region that was to become Normandy began when it was recorded that the Vikings first entered the Seine estuary. The abbeys at Jumièges and St Wandrille were sacked in 841, and it is recorded that the latter paid 26 pounds of silver for the release of 68 prisoners. There was an escalation of Viking involvement in north-western France when they over-wintered in the Seine valley for the first time in 851. Reputedly, two bishops of Bayeux, Suplicius (844) and Baltfrid (858), were martyred by the Vikings, and c.855 the Scandinavians captured the regional capital of Rouen. It is symptomatic of the havoc that the Vikings were able to inflict on the vulnerable monastic institutions along the Seine, which were the chief chroniclers of early Viking activity in the region, that the accounts of events ceased in the second half of the ninth century as the monasteries themselves were suppressed.

For more than a century the Danes attacked the Empire; not only in its weaker outlying territories, but also in its heart lands, in the valleys of the rivers flowing into the North Sea and in the Loire Valley where the Frankish traditions of the Empire were strongest. It was here that the monasteries were thickly planted and, enriched by two centuries of royal patronage, presented an almost irresistible target for the Vikings. The imperial family's political troubles after Charlemagne's death did not help to co-ordinate resistance to the new enemies, and even the energetic emperor Charles the Bald (861–2) was reduced to employing one band of enemies to fight another. The invaders' skill on the water, their surprise attacks and their ability to operate in small bands made them difficult for the Franks to deal with except at a local level, and it was here that the imperial government was at its weakest.

The Franks did not respond in the same way as the Anglo-Saxons to Viking attacks; there is, for instance, little evidence of a co-ordinated use of defensive works. Some linear earthworks, such as the Hague Dyke which extended across the northern Cotentin peninsula, were constructed or reinforced, and defensive earthworks of one form or another sprang up across the region, but there appears to have been no systematic network of defended towns as found in England. The invaders were not faced by the co-ordinated resistance which developed under the auspices of the Wessex monarchy in the later years of the ninth century. Despite the energetic efforts of some of the Carolingian kings, effective defence was increasingly organised independently of the monarchy. What this actually involved in terms of the types of fortification to be found in the territory which was later to become Normandy is an area where archaeological investigation has only just begun. The persistence of the raids and the progressive dissolution of the powers of the Frankish monarchy meant that both the kings and the local men who were in the process of acquiring authority began to offer political compromises similar in character to the Treaty of Wedmore.

Other embryonic Norse colonies in the lower Loire and in Ireland failed. Normandy was thus by far the most successful of the European mainland 'colonies', several of which had already floundered before 911. One of these, on the lower Weiser, lasted for less than 30 years (826–52), another in Frisia around Walcheren survived for just over 40 (841–85). A colony at Nantes planted in 919 was eliminated in 937. Only in England had dense Viking colonisation in the Danelaw enabled the Scandinavians to bring about a major change in the history of the whole country, but even here it was not because it survived as an independent political unit. Normandy alone survived several political and military crises to become one of the major feudal principalities within the old Frankish kingdom.

The Bretons

There were other threats to the empire in the west. Flanders had been created as a result of military expansion by count Baldwin II between 883 and 918, from a much smaller base given to his father, count Baldwin I, by King Charles the Bald, and was developing into a potential threat to the empire. Even more significant was the danger from Brittany. Brittany, for most of its history, enjoyed a separate existence from mainstream France and had never been fully absorbed into the Carolingian Empire. The Bretons, with strong Celtic roots, were ethnically distinct from the Franks, but their close proximity to the empire meant that they were heavily influenced by Frankish customs and institutions, particularly in the eastern part of their kingdom. Immediately to the east of Brittany, the region known as the Breton or Neustrian March had been established by the Franks in an unsuccessful attempt to contain not the Vikings, but the Bretons. In Charlemagne's time this had extended from Calais in the north to the Breton borders in the south; the boundaries had fluctuated in the ninth century as the powers of neighbouring principalities had waxed and waned.

In 862 Charles the Bald granted the March to Robert the Strong with the specific intention of containing the Bretons. This clearly did not work, as in 867 the Bretons were granted possession of the Cotentin and Avranchin regions of what became Normandy. Significantly, the agreement by which this was executed has a remarkable similarity to the grant later made to Rollo the Viking in 911. It conferred all royal rights on Robert, except that of nominating bishops. Subsequently, the Bretons moved even further east into the area around Bayeux, but were unable to consolidate their hold on the region. After about 850 the situation in western Francia became increasingly unstable, not purely because of Breton, or even Viking, pressure, but also because of the divisions within the decaying Western Empire. These divisions enabled Brittany to flourish politically and its rulers to adopt the title of king. Initially, the creation of Normandy did not contain the Bretons and King Alan II Barbetorte (936–52) was able to push back the Normans almost as far as Rouen. Brittany was to remain a major threat to the duchy right up to the middle of the eleventh century.

The Creation of Normandy

One account relates that in 897 Charles III (the Simple), king of the western Franks, was dissuaded from ceding territory to the Vikings on the grounds that it would be wrong to ally himself with pagans. However, if this is true he was soon to change his mind. Charles had earned the epithet 'Simple' (*simplex*) not because of his stupidity, but because of his good nature and honest disposition. Yet according to the chronicler Dudo, an early eleventh-century canon of St Quintin, it was after Charles had defeated a mixed band of warriors led by a Viking war-lord called Rollo at Chartres that Normandy came into being in 911. Rollo, who was, according to tradition, of noble Norwegian ancestry, was persuaded to make peace, become a Christian and stand guard for the Franks against the Vikings and Bretons in the Seine Valley (**6**).

There is little authentic information about Rollo; we have to depend heavily on Dudo who constructed a history of the principality of Normandy, the oldest surviving work of its kind. Dudo also recounts a tale of Rollo's legendary predecessor as leader of the Norsemen, Hastings, but Dudo's record has to be interpreted with extreme caution as much of it seems to be fictitious. However, it does seem that in 911, at St Clair-sur-Epte in the Vexin on the eastern boundary of Normandy, Charles and Rollo concluded an agreement by which the Norsemen were ceded 'certain districts (*pagi*) bordering the sea coast, along with the city of Rouen'. According to Dudo, the counties of Normandy pertaining to the Archbishopric of Rouen extended over approximately the same region that had previously comprised the Gallo-Roman province of *Lugdunensis Secunda*. Rouen's Roman walls were still standing, although its location on the north bank of the river Seine meant that it was always vulnerable to attack from the river. In return for the grant, Rollo agreed to protect the region and it is further recorded that he and his followers were converted to Christianity.

The land granted to Rollo was given in full ownership (*in alodo et in fundo*) in order to emphasise that, from the very beginning, the Norman rulers were remarkably independent of the French Kings. Dudo's colourful account included a story about Rollo's refusal to bend his knee before King Charles. Instead, one of the soldiers was delegated to take part in the ceremony, and in his attempt to kiss the king's foot without bending down he sent the Frankish monarch tumbling backwards. Dudo does, however, admit that both Rollo and his son, William Longsword, did homage to the Frankish king. He records that Rollo was given Charles' daughter Gisela in marriage, a story not substantiated by any other source.

Only the central area of the Seine, consisting of the *pagi* of Talou, Caux, Roumois and part of the Vexin and Evrecin, was given in the original treaty. In 924, Charles' successor King Ralph ceded Bayeux and Maine, the area of central and southern Normandy, to Rollo. In 933, William I, Rollo's son, received 'the land of the Bretons situated on the sea coast', i.e. Avranchin and Cotentin, that land which the Bretons had earlier acquired from the young Normandy. Thus by 933 Norman territory roughly conformed to its 1066 extent (**7**).

As we have seen, the Treaty of St Clair-sur-Epte was not the first attempt by the Carolingians to contain the Vikings by harnessing their energy in support of the Empire, but it was the one that was responsible for creating the duchy of Normandy. The grant of lands to Rollo and his followers should be interpreted as a typical response by the harassed western European ruling classes to the Viking presence. The Treaty of St Clair-sur-Epte

6   *Nineteenth-century statue of Count Rollo, the Viking founder of Normandy in Rouen*

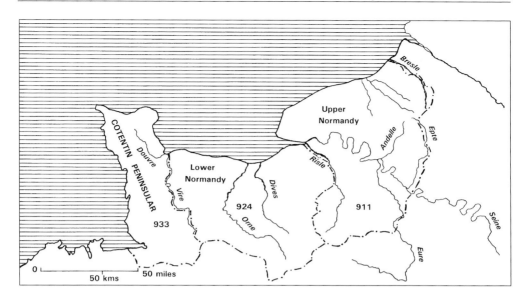

7   *Map showing the development of Normandy in the tenth century*

was made between a Frankish king whose successors might easily seek to overthrow it and a Viking chief who could not guarantee to control the new settlers. What was to become the duchy of Normandy was founded within a society which was itself highly unstable and in the midst of profound social change. In other words, the creation of Normandy was an act of political expediency, which might or might not have been expected to last. The founder members of the Norman ducal dynasty, Rollo (911–31) and his son William Longsword (931–42), adopted the title of Count of Rouen. Rollo's grandson, Richard I, styled himself 'marquis of the Normans' and referred to his 'kingdom'. But it was not until 1015 that Richard's son and successor, Richard II, styled himself duke and patrician, asserting his right to control the church and appoint counts under him.

Professor le Patourel has distinguished between the 'Viking' stage in the development of Normandy, which was characterised by conquest, plunder and piracy, and the succeeding 'feudal' stage towards the end of the tenth century, when the institutions of the 'duchy' began to emerge. The early 'dukes' defeated other rival groups of settlers, exercising their powers of banishment and gaining and retaining considerable amounts of land and wealth. But they also inherited and revived the powers of earlier Carolingian counts, which gave them rights over forests, coinage, castles and taxation.

The new duchy was subject to internal and external problems from the time of its creation, particularly in the west where there was pressure from both Bretons and Scandinavians. Additionally, the inhabitants of Bayeux, who were placed under Norman rule in 924, revolted in 925. Despite such problems, almost from the beginning Normans were active outside the duchy and it is recorded that Normans from Rouen fought alongside the army of Charles the Simple in the region around Beauvais in 923. In 924 the

Normans sacked Amiens and Arras to the north-east of the duchy and moved as far eastwards as Noyon, and there is even some evidence for Norman activity in Brittany itself. It appears that, initially, Norman rulers extended their control to those regions which they were able to subdue, a policy that William the Conqueror was later to adopt in Wales. In 925 Rollo was defeated in the east at Eu, a place that lay on what was to become the Norman frontier. Rollo died c.931 and was succeeded by his son, William Longsword (931–42) (**colour plate 3**). Conversion to Christianity in the first half of the tenth century was often superficial and did not immediately satisfy the Viking appetite for land. On his deathbed it is understood that Rollo made both benefactions to Christian churches and human sacrifice. Such was the scale of conversion that the Archbishop of Rouen, helped by the Archbishop of Rheims, undertook the process of conversion using a special handbook consisting of 23 texts.

There appears to have been an uprising in 933–4, led by a wealthy Scandinavian called Rioul, which was put down by William. Relatively little is known of the second Norman leader, but it is clear that his reign saw the accelerated adoption of Frankish practices. William married a Christian wife, Lutegarde, the daughter of Count Herbert II of Vermandois, who brought with her a dowry organised along Frankish lines. Also, the Rouen mint was revived directly on the lines of its Carolingian predecessor. However, it suppressed all reference on its coins to the Frankish kings, replacing them with William's own name. William also seems to have started the construction of a palace at Fécamp with the use of slaves, along the lines of those built by his fellow northern French princes (**8a** and **b**).

Several aspects of the Carolingian Church were restored in the first half of the tenth century. Lands were restored to the church and Bayeux was refounded with an abbot from Cluny (founded 909) at its head. St Ouen, Jumièges and Mont St Michel all received new grants. Other signs of restoration included the return of relics to, and refoundation of, the monastery of St Ouen in Rouen, and the return of its estates which had been taken over by the Vikings. William Longsword oversaw the restoration of the monasteries of Jumièges and, under Richard I, Mont St Michel, St-Wandrille and Fécamp.

William's murder in 942 at the hands of Arnulf of Flanders threw the young principality into chaos. He was succeeded by his young son Richard I (942–96), the issue of his union with his Breton mistress. Between 942 and 946 Normandy was subjected to the same pressures that destroyed other Viking principalities. Scandinavian war-bands intervened in force, and a certain Harold established an independent power-base at Bayeux, while there was also a reaction to the wholesale conversion to Christianity within the province led by a pagan-Norman called Turmod. In addition, there were intermittent attempts at reconquest by the Frankish kings, notably under King Louis IV, but most of these failed due to deep-seated rivalries within the Western Empire. There were other conflicts, but these were the result of local uprisings in Normandy and external forays against the Franks. After 965, following a concerted attack on Rouen from Flanders and Anjou, Richard appears to have abandoned his attacks against the French kings and concentrated on the consolidation of Normandy in a policy that undoubtedly contributed greatly to the survival of the principality. The young Richard survived this disturbed phase at the beginning of his rule and went on to provide relatively stable government for most of the rest of the tenth century.

8 (a)   Exterior view of a ducal palace at Fécamp

The Viking Legacy

There has been much discussion about the scale of Viking migration to France in the tenth century. Although place name evidence indicates a significant infiltration in certain limited areas, undoubtedly most of the population of Normandy remained Frankish. Administratively and culturally, Rollo and his followers were rapidly assimilated into the Frankish world. The language of power remained solidly Carolingian, e.g. *regnum, dux, comes* and *fidelitas*. The Normans collected parcels of rights, once exercised on behalf of Carolingian rulers, and exploited them to their own advantage. It was such rights that provided the fiscal foundations of Norman ducal power. According to tradition, the new Norman leaders readily married into Frankish society. Rollo married Poppa, the daughter of the Frankish Count of Bayeux, and William Longsword married the daughter of another Frankish count. Government by regional assembly, which lay at the heart of Scandinavian administration, never took root on Norman soil, but nevertheless, although there was considerable institutional continuity there was also a great rupture in the ruling class.

The Scandinavian tongue survived for longer in the Danelaw of England than in Normandy, assisted by both by the scale of Viking migration and the similarity of the Anglo-Saxon and Scandinavian languages, but this was not so in northern France where the speaking of Frankish was enforced and a form of early French developed. There is a well known story of how William Longsword sent his son to Bayeux to learn Scandinavian as it was no longer spoken in Rouen, where it was considered to be a base language. Certain Scandinavian traditions did survive, however; eleventh-century dukes had the right to exile (*ullac*), there were exclusive powers over murder and assault, maritime laws were maintained (giving rights over shipwrecks), there was 'partible' inheritance, and

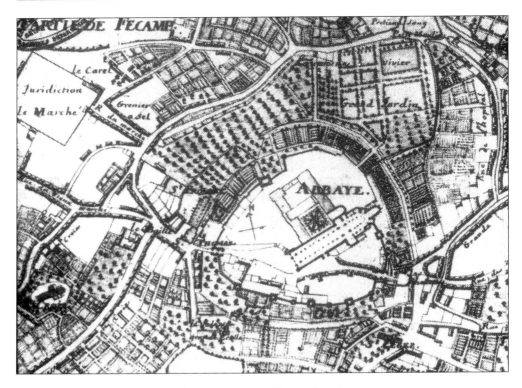

8 (b)   Eighteenth-century map showing Fécamp Abbey and precinct

there was the very strong authoritarian nature of the Norman government which showed a sharp distinction between warriors and farmers. Although some parts of Normandy were still Norse speaking as late as the twelfth century, the Normans quickly became Franks in culture, the language combining elements from both northern and native elements for the purpose of conducting everyday life.

Place name evidence suggests that, in addition to settlers arriving directly from Scandinavia, Normandy received colonists who had dwelt for a time in other territories. For instance, the existence of place names containing an Anglo-Saxon element in the Pays de Caux suggests the migration of Scandinavians and others who had lived for some time in England, while Celtic toponyms in the north of the Cotentin peninsular indicate Irish-Scandinavian colonisation there, a pattern of movement which parallels that from Ireland to northern England. Hybrid place names are common, for example Scandinavian personal names ending in *ville*, such as Tocqueville (Tokis ville), or Osbert's-ville (Auberville). Another common Scandinavian place name element was *bec* — stream. The heaviest concentration of Scandinavian place names was in Cotentin and the maritime area of upper Normandy (**9**). The place name evidence points to heavy early colonisation in coastal areas, but indicates the Scandinavian take-over of existing villages for the most part rather than the establishment of new settlements. In the region around Bayeux, place name evidence indicates that the Scandinavian colonisation was in marginal land rather

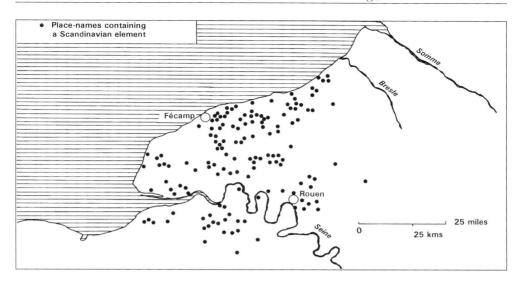

9   Map showing Scandinavian place names in Normandy

than in heavily settled areas. After the initial phase of settlement by Vikings there seems to have been relatively little colonisation. Even in those areas with a high density of Scandinavian place names, such as in the Cotentin peninsula or the Pays de Caux, nowhere do they outnumber pre-existing Frankish names. On the other hand, Scandinavian personal names became fashionable and continued to be used after the language had ceased to be spoken, and even in the eleventh century Norman aristocrats are sometimes known to have carried both a Scandinavian and a French name, for instance, Thorsteinn and Richard. Many Normans who travelled to southern Italy carried Scandinavian names such as Toroldus, Torstenns, Osmundus and Osbernus, but abandoned them in favour of Carolingian German names within a generation or so.

The Normans did not abandon all their Scandinavian characteristics. One anecdote recounts that, on becoming Count of Rouen, Rollo took over royal lands and proceeded to reduce the region he had been given to a desert and then handed it over to his followers. There was a Viking expedition in 935, fitted out at Rouen, which pillaged in the vicinity of Therouanne, and on a number of other occasions in the tenth century the Normans allowed Vikings to use their ports as bases for attacks on England. There is even some evidence for the Normans hiring Viking warriors for their expeditions. On one occasion at Therouanne it is recorded that the approach of King Ralph's French army caused the Scandinavian raiders to strangle their prisoners and try to make a quick escape. Up until c.1025, the Norman rulers maintained Rouen as an open city for Viking raiders and profited considerably through the provision of necessities to the pirates, although they had abandoned the Rouen slave market by about 1000. The last reference to the Rouen slave trade is late tenth century when Rouen was referred to as 'a pirates' mart'.

Contacts across the Scandinavian north proved to be long-lasting. Duke Richard II (996–1026) made an agreement with Sven Forkbeard, King of Denmark, to divide the loot that had been taken in the latter's invasion of England following the defeat of Æthelred the Unready. At about the same time, men from Normandy appear alongside Scandinavians at the battle of Clontarf (1014) in Ireland, and an Irishman, sold into slavery at Corbridge in Northumberland, after a long journey, located his wife at Le Vaudreuil in Normandy.

The result of the grant made to Rollo in 911 on the river Epte was the creation of a new political unit in Northern France. Seminal to any understanding of this region's history in the tenth and eleventh centuries is an estimate of the effects which the Scandinavian settlements had on the society of the province. A beguiling image of a vigorous Viking society, which sustained a continuity of aggression over a century and a half, provides a simplistic explanation for the expansion of the Normans from c.1020 onwards. Social and political change is, however, far more complicated than this. The 155 years between 911 and 1066 represent a complex period in which the Scandinavian settlers shed most of the characteristics associated with the Vikings and changed into the inhabitants of a well-organised territorial principality. As the Norsemen gradually adopted Frankish culture they were themselves thought of as Franks, although as late as 987, at the acclamation of Hugh Capet as King of France at Noyen, the Normans were referred to as Danes. The text beneath a scene in the Bayeux Tapestry (probably executed in the 1070s) reads: 'Here the English and the *Franks* fell in battle.' By the middle of the eleventh century the Normans had changed their fighting techniques so much that they had no fleet to speak of and had to build and requisition one for the invasion of England. A few years later, the chronicler Guilbert expressed the view that Bohémond, ruler of southern Italy, was a Frank because he came from Normandy, 'which is part of Francia'.

The main problem for Rollo and his successors was not with his own followers but, as in other places in Europe at this time, former subordinates who had developed their positions of power independently of him. From the end of the tenth century castles began to be built in Normandy, marking the militarisation of the Duchy. With the nobility becoming more organised, private warfare spread despite the comparatively strong rule of the dukes.

During the tenth century there was little to distinguish the Norman duchy from its neighbours, with the exception, perhaps, of its Scandinavian complexion. It is a century for which we have relatively little surviving documentary, archaeological or architectural evidence, and what we are able to deduce does not give much indication of the dramatic success on the political and military stage that Normandy was to enjoy during the eleventh century. On a political front, Normandy continued to operate a perennially changing network of alliances, often linked by intermarriage within other northern French principalities. In particular, their relationship with the Capetian kings was of fundamental importance.

Our sources for the reconstruction of tenth-century Normandy are relatively sparse, but when we move into the eleventh century sources become plentiful, a fact which itself reflects changed social conditions. In the year 1000 Normandy remained rather backward, dominated by wealthy rulers, and with the church largely untouched by movements of reform which were influential in other regions, and an aristocracy as yet unaffected by structural changes which were taking place elsewhere in France. Normandy arrived in an eleventh century in which the dominant powers were the territorial rulers of former Carolingian lands whose local independence had evolved through the later tenth century into a harshly competitive and exceptionally brutal world.

2 Normandy in the first half of the eleventh century

During the eleventh century Normandy finally broke its strong cultural and political links with Scandinavia and began contact with southern Europe and the Mediterranean. In 1018 there were the first indications of a military Norman presence in southern Italy, and Roger de Tosny's campaign against the Moslems in Spain dates from about the same time. The Scandinavian Conquest of England by Sven Forkbeard and his son Cnut appears to have marked the end of these northern links when the Normans sided with the Anglo-Saxons in support of Æthelred. This episode was followed by the English pretender to the throne Edward the Confessor seeking exile in Duke Richard II's court in Normandy.

By the end of the tenth century, Normandy already had many of the governmental characteristics of contemporary French territorial principalities. Many Carolingian governmental institutions and their territorial boundaries survived the Viking period; this has been a source of particular comment among historians who observe that the duchy's early Norman rulers adopted existing institutions in France as resolutely as they were later to do in England and in the Mediterranean.

By the millennium the western Carolingian empire had disintegrated, but the new Capetian king, based on Paris, had inherited its legacy of sovereignty. North-eastern France had evolved into a number of virtually autonomous principalities: Flanders, Ponthieu, Maine, Brittany and Normandy, while to the east lay the embryonic Capetian kingdom with whom these principalities allied themselves from time to time. In theory the individual principalities owed allegiance to the French crown, but in practice at this stage most of them were more powerful than the monarchy itself. During the first half of the eleventh century Normandy established itself as a well-organised state with a powerful army. Norman military forces enabled its dukes to participate effectively in the politics of north-western Europe, and intervene both politically and militarily in the affairs of other principalities. Thus in the eleventh century, building on a basically Carolingian demographic and administrative framework, Normandy was able to develop a new and powerful aristocracy, church, monasticism and culture. 'As a result, the Normans had produced a new state and new society which no longer belonged to the Scandinavian world, but was in the forefront of the military and cultural development of the French' (Ralph Davis).

The long rule of Richard I came to an end in 996 when he was succeeded by his son Richard II, the first Norman ruler to style himself 'Duke'; the adoption of this title enabled Richard to join the small élite group of Frankish dukes. Significantly, however, the Capetian kings of France refused to acknowledge the title until they themselves became 'dukes of Normandy' in 1204. Duke Richard I (996–1026) married Judith, the daughter of Duke Conan I of Brittany, thus forging an alliance with the old enemy. Richard proved himself to be a reforming ruler both in secular and ecclesiastical affairs. During Richard II's period as duke (1026–7), Normandy acquired much of the complexion of the duchy to be seen at the time of the invasion of England. Richard II died without male heirs, in what some contemporaries regarded as suspicious circumstances.

Richard II, because he had been a reforming leader, was followed as duke by his younger brother Robert (1027–35), who was betrothed to the daughter of King Cnut but who died at Nicae in Asia Minor on return from pilgrimage to Jerusalem (**colour plate 5**). Robert's short reign and long absence from Normandy was characterised by political and military disturbances and disputes with the church, a condition which deteriorated further in the early years of the rule of his successor, his bastard son, William II (1035–87). William's eventual success in quelling opposition both within and outside the duchy enabled him to establish one of the most powerful principalities in Europe. Essentially, it was these three eleventh-century dukes who fashioned a Normandy which was capable of defeating and ruling Anglo-Saxon England. Yet we know relatively little about the first two dukes and, perhaps surprisingly, despite the seminal role he played in eleventh-century European history, our knowledge of William himself is limited.

The Norman army

The rise of Normandy as a powerful principality was paralleled by its neighbours, Anjou, Brittany and Flanders. In each of these proto-states their princes established a powerful infrastructure based on fortresses and new centres of power. Thus, ostensibly, there was little to distinguish Normandy from its continental neighbours during the first half of the eleventh century. Although the re-organisation of civil and ecclesiastical institutions was of considerable importance in establishing this power, it was the army that was the Normans' strongest asset. The value of efficient military organisation within the context of the Frankish world should not be underestimated, and the Norman dukes owed much of their influence to their strength in this department. Military organisation was a priority reflected by the images of the Bayeux Tapestry in its depiction of the preparations for the invasion of 1066. The Tapestry gives particular prominence to the organisation of military equipment and supplies — helmets, hauberks, swords, lances, axes, barrels and skins of wine and the assembling and building of the invasion fleet which, quite exceptionally, was completed within a period of eight months (**10**).

By the eleventh century, despite its Viking origins, Normandy essentially fought with land-based armies. By definition, the fleet was of only limited importance in its constant quarrels with its neighbours. It is widely acknowledged that Norman use of cavalry was a significant contributory factor in their success at Hastings and their love of horses was legendary. This was reflected in the depiction of equestrian activity on the Bayeux Tapestry. The Norman cavalry used a horse known as a *destrier*, which was reputed to be nimble even when carrying a heavily armed rider, and which was used to effect in a number of campaigns. The Normans not only trained horses in war-like conditions but also imported war-horses from Arab Spain and North Africa, and used them to breed in parks especially created for the purpose (**11**).

10   *Norman military preparations for the conquest of England as depicted on the Bayeux Tapestry*

During the tenth century Normandy was controlled by a count with a number of followers, but when Richard II adopted the title of duke he appointed a number of subordinate counts in militarily important areas — for example, at Avranches in the Cotentin peninsula, to guard the Breton frontier, at Ivrey by the county of Blois-Chartres, and at Eu near the frontier with Flanders. Without exception, these counts were not drawn from the ranks of local aristocrats, but were all directly related to him. This, to a large extent, is what gave Normandy its considerable political unity, although the landed wealth of the duke himself, and his absolute control of the church in the form of the right to appoint bishoprics and to found abbeys, was also a major element.

From the late tenth century the Normans recruited skilled soldiers from outside their province. When William the Conqueror brought knights from Brittany, Flanders, Artois, and Picardy into his army for the invasion of England he was only following the policy of his predecessors. Families such as the Tosnys and the Bellêmes, who were Frankish, and the Taisons from Anjou were recruited into the military service of the Norman dukes. Many of these 'foreign' knights were rapidly assimilated into the Norman aristocracy; indeed, few of the great baronial families who were subsequently to feature so prominently in Anglo-Norman affairs had acquired their Norman lands before 1030. By the middle of the eleventh century there were few, if any, Norman barons whose Viking blood had not been diluted by marriage, and there were many who had no Viking ancestry at all. The view that Normandy essentially recreated itself in the eleventh century, largely

11   *Norman cavalryman from twelfth-century document, showing high saddle and stirrups*

through the inward migration of influential and powerful people from elsewhere in France and outside, is one held by many scholars. There is, however, a counter opinion that, while recognising the contribution made by the newcomers, claims that many of the families which figure prominently in the eleventh century were already in the duchy in the tenth century, but that their presence is masked by the paucity of early documentation.

The Norman church

The Norman dukes treated the church within their duchy as another arm of government. Next to the army the church was the most important institution that contributed to Norman success. Just as the reorganisation of the Norman aristocracy in the eleventh century was to provide a model for what was to happen later in England, so too the reform of the Norman church was to play a vital role as a model in the subsequent creation of Anglo-Norman England. As secular and ecclesiastical boundaries were largely coincidental, Normandy was well-placed for a fusion of the church and state. The process of strengthening the church also involved the introduction of outsiders in the early eleventh century. Subsequently, the churchmen of eleventh-century Normandy were to establish a formidable reputation as reformers, whose scholarship won a European-wide recognition.

Although the Scandinavians had embraced Christianity and began re-establishing the monasteries, which only a few years earlier they had been plundering, the tenth-century Norman church was far from distinguished. Apart from the community of Mont-St-Michel on the border between Normandy and Brittany, which had developed a considerable flair for collecting and copying manuscripts, there was little evidence of artistic or architectural achievement in tenth-century Normandy. Indeed, there were even some signs of decadence; the Anglo-Norman historian Orderic Vitalis recorded that the early Norman priests of Danish extraction were addicted to both arms and concubines, and that when ecclesiastical reforms were being introduced they were more willing to give up the former than the latter.

By 990, the diocesan framework of the province of Rouen had been reconstituted. It consisted of the six suffragan bishoprics of Avranches, Coutances, Bayeux, Sees, Lisieux and Evreux (**12**). In the far west the bishops of Coutances were unable to take up residence in their cathedral city for some decades thereafter. The decisive development in the Norman church came in 1001 when Duke Richard II, inspired by ecclesiastical reforms further south in Burgundy, decided to replace the secular clerks at Fécamp with a monastic community. Fécamp was the duke's power base in upper Normandy, where he already had a palace. The duke looked for help from outside the duchy and succeeded in attracting a noted ecclesiastical reformer to Normandy in the form of an Italian called William of Volpiano (or William of Dijon), who was at that time abbot of St Benign at Dijon. William had been trained at the great Benedictine abbey of Cluny where he had been responsible for introducing radical reforms; once established at Fécamp, he used the abbey there as a base to strengthen the church throughout the duchy. Duke Richard II endowed Fécamp with a large number of rural churches, and also gave it far-reaching privileges including exemption from external authority, both ducal and ecclesiastical. Fécamp abbey was also allowed to organise the ordination of priests, which enabled it to

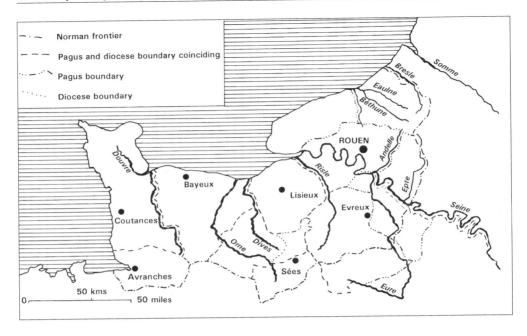

Norman frontier

Pagus and diocese boundary coinciding

Pagus boundary

Diocese boundary

12   *Map showing the relationship between eleventh-century ecclesiastical boundaries and Roman administrative divisions in Normandy*

become a training school for clergy as well as a centre for evangelism. Earlier, Richard himself had tried but failed to bring monks from Cluny to Fécamp, and apparently even William of Volpiano at first demurred, objecting that he understood that the Normans were more likely to devastate than build the temples of the lord.

William's principal Norman agent was a man called Thierry (d.1027), who was reputedly related to the Montgomery family which had emerged as part of the 'new aristocracy' in the 1030s and 1040s. Thierry, who became prior at Fécamp, had been the abbot of both Jumièges and Mont-St-Michel from 1017 and 1023 respectively. He contributed to the reorganisation of the dioceses of Bayeux and Coutances by acquiring revenue-earning estates for them, by establishing parish churches for village communities, and by assisting in the foundation of new monasteries (**13**). His work had a significant impact both on the quality of the religious life of the Norman church and on the influence of the church on the community. The number of monasteries in Normandy increased from five in 1000 to over 30 by 1066, and it is believed that William of Volpiano was involved in the foundation of over 20 of these (**colour plate 4**).

In addition to William, there were other important foreign recruits to the Norman church. These included another Italian, a cleric called Lanfranc who transformed the abbey at Bec from a place of relative obscurity to become one of the most famous foundations in Europe. Lanfranc was born in Pavia c.1005 and settled in Normandy c.1039. He founded a school at Avranches and three years later entered the monastery at Bec, becoming prior there in 1045. Pupils from throughout Europe were attracted to Bec,

13   The ornate exterior of Thaon parish church near Caen (twelfth century)

the most notable being two other Italians, Anselm of Lucca (the future Pope Alexander II) and Anselm of Aosta. The latter was one of the greatest intellects of the early middle ages and eventually succeeded Lanfranc as Archbishop of Canterbury (1093–1109), although his prelateship in England was to be characterised by political controversy both under William Rufus and Henry I.

Other monasteries also came under the control of foreign abbots — Italians like John of Fruttuaria at Fécamp, Suppo of Fruttuaria at Mont-St-Michel, and Isembard Teutonicus at Holy Trinity. Rouen, as the Norman capital, became a centre of prestige, wealth, learning and spiritual excellence and provided direct links with the great monasteries of Burgundy, northern Italy and with Rome itself. Lanfranc acted as William's agent in developing and strengthening the episcopacy and fashioning it as a tool of government. Lanfranc appointed William's nominees to vacant sees; the duke's half-brother Odo to Bayeux in 1049, although he was little more than a boy at the time and well below the canonical age of 30 required to become a bishop; Hugh to Liseux (1049) and Geoffrey to Coutances (1048). By these appointments he was able to ensure control of the allegiance of the bishops and effective political control of their estates. One source also records that Lanfranc interceded with the papacy on William's behalf over his disputed marriage to Matilda, although the frequently-told story that he travelled to Rome to present the duke's case appears to be untrue.

Later, as prior of William's abbey of St Stephens in Caen, Lanfranc (1063–70) was to play an important role in helping to develop Caen as William's alternative urban power base to Rouen (**colour plate 6**). By the 1050s and 1060s new abbey churches were being built at Mont-St-Michel, Remy, Jumièges and Caen. Although these new churches relied heavily on Burgundian sources, they displayed the beginnings of a new distinctive Norman style of architecture (**14a** and **b**). The revival of the importance of the episcopacy was followed by the construction of new cathedrals on a scale commensurate with that of the monasteries and, following on from the cathedrals and abbeys, parish churches were built or reconstructed in stone in the new 'Norman' Romanesque style (**15a** and **b**). The term 'Norman', used to describe the neo-classical style found in England from the time of the Conquest to about 1200, is only used in Britain. In Normandy it is known as Romanesque or, more properly, as 'Roman', as indeed it is throughout much of Western Europe where it was adopted. In France, the term 'Romanesque' tends to be associated with nineteenth-century replicas of Norman architecture and, most importantly, the work of Viollet le Duc (1814–79), the French architect and writer, whose restorations included the Cité of Carcassonne and St Ouen at Rouen.

Norman society

It was the emergence of the new aristocracy with families such as the Beaumonts, the Bohuns and the Warennes, which effectively marked the real break between the sub-Carolingian and the authentic Norman period. By the middle of the eleventh century the newly established ruling group was operating within the framework of territorial feudalism. In the middle decades of the eleventh century, during the rule of Duke William II (nicknamed 'William the Bastard' before the Battle of Hastings), Norman society had adopted the feudal structure that operated in many other parts of France. Serfs were tied to the land, the ownership of estates was becoming hereditary and, in return for land, barons, bishops and abbots were required to provide the duke with specific quotas of knights for up to 40 days in each year.

The Norman duke was by far the richest man in his duchy and he had tighter control over his subjects and their economy than any other European prince. The estates of his barons were kept deliberately small and the earth-and-wooden (motte and bailey) castles and defensive enclosures, which were built on many of those estates, could not be constructed without a licence and had to be surrendered on demand. Within each county the courts, the army, the collection of revenues and the maintenance of order were under the control of the viscounts who were directly appointed by the duke.

Despite the spread of feudalism, which in theory tied men to the land, greater mobility within Europe was a feature of eleventh-century Frankish society. Normans were prominent within this movement, largely because of the disturbed conditions, which prevailed within the duchy from c.1025 when Normandy was convulsed by warfare within its ruling classes. This was symptomatic of the form of feudal revolution which involved, as in other regions in France, castle building and the subjugation of previously free landholders. It created conditions which undoubtedly fuelled migration from the duchy to southern Europe and to Italy in particular. What began as a trickle of criminals, disaffected knights and pilgrims in the first decades of the eleventh century, developed into a stream of younger sons and their followers, eager for the spoils from distant regions,

14(a)   The east end of the twelfth-century abbey church at Cerisy-La-Forêt

14(b) Interior of William the Conqueror's abbey church of St Stephen's, Caen

*15(a) Ruins of Jumièges abbey church built in the eleventh century, contemporary with Edward the Confessor's Westminster Abbey church (see **colour plate 10**)*

where conflicts between neighbouring petty states were endemic and where the prizes for the successful were enormous.

As a sequel to this phase, William the Conqueror's pacification of the duchy after 1050 was based on a policy of mobilising the Norman barons in wars against neighbouring powers. The Normans brought military methods based on cavalry and castles to their new lands, which were superior to those of the people they were fighting. Everywhere they ventured, the Normans took with them the moveable institutions of lordship which gave cohesion to the groups of warriors who carried out their conquests. The acquisition of land by lords was almost always followed by the transfer of much of it to their vassals in return for military service. Military feudalism enabled William to dominate the duchy and to mobilise Normandy on frequent occasions.

The growth of towns

One of the features of economic and political success in north-western France at this time was in the development of towns. Rouen was by far the largest and most prosperous of Norman towns. Indeed, within what later became France it was probably second only to Paris in importance by the first half of the eleventh century. Its location, on the navigable Seine, meant that it had links with Paris and the interior of France as well as with coastal Normandy and beyond. It was the ecclesiastical and secular capital of the Norman world as well as being a major urban centre in its own right. It had a mint which dated back to

15(b) The western front of St George's abbey church at Boscherville. A plain façade with twin flanking towers is typical of late eleventh-century Norman architecture

Carolingian times, and it had been the centre of the Viking slave trade during the tenth century. However, those very factors that made it important were also its weakness. It was vulnerable to attack from the river, and to compensate for this the Norman dukes developed other power centres such as Fécamp and Caen.

Norman urban life was flourishing by the middle of the eleventh century with Rouen and the episcopal towns, most of which had Roman origins, forming the basis for administration and commerce. William the Conqueror deliberately fostered the development of the town of Caen between Bayeux and Rouen on an island at the confluence of the rivers Orne and Odon. William chose to develop Caen as a military stronghold with significant strategic advantages over Rouen; one of its principal attractions was that it was less vulnerable to attack than the ancient capital. It also lay in the very heart of the narrow belt of Jurassic limestone, an excellent building material, which provided the source of Caen stone for the constructions of castles, churches, monasteries and secular buildings in Normandy and later on in England (**16a**).

During the early part of his reign William's control of the whole of Normandy was precarious, in particular until after the battle of Val-ès-Dunes in 1047. At one stage he may even have lost control of his capital at Rouen and been obliged to rely on Caen as his power base in lower Normandy. By the end of the first quarter of the eleventh century a cluster of villages had formed at what was to become Caen, and the importance of this site was evidently recognised in 1047 when it was chosen as the meeting place of the council which proclaimed the Truce of God. Thenceforward, William, who appreciated the

16(a) The massive surviving ramparts of the castle at Caen which originated under William the Conqueror and were modified on many later occasions

strategic and commercial advantages of this position, took positive action to foster the growth of an urban agglomeration on the site, providing it with stone walls, a castle, and making it one of his principal residences. The regard he had for it is displayed today in the two magnificent abbey churches which remain the glory of the town, and it is significant that on his death William was to be buried not, like his ancestors, at Rouen or Fécamp, but in his abbey of St Stephen at Caen. The Abbey of Holy Trinity (Abbaye-aux-Dames) was constructed for William's duchess, Matilda, and was to be her eventual burial place. It lay on high ground to the west of the castle (**16b**). These two fine abbeys dominated the city and contributed to its title of 'Athens of the North' before it was largely destroyed during the Second World War. Although not an episcopal city, Caen rose during his lifetime to become the second town in Normandy, and its early growth owes more to William the Conqueror than to anyone else. The rise of Caen during the Conqueror's reign was symptomatic of his success in stamping his own personality on the duchy and in finally integrating upper and lower Normandy into a single political unit.

Duke William II (1035–87)

William II, or William the Conqueror as he became known after the Battle of Hastings, was born at Falaise (**colour plate 7**), some 30 km to the south-east of Caen, in 1027–8.

16(b) Holy Trinity (Abbaye-aux-Dames), at Caen, built before the conquest of England for William's Queen Matilda

He was the illegitimate son of Duke Robert I (or Robert the Magnificent as he was popularly known) and Herlève, reputedly a tanner's daughter (**17a** and **b**). Robert's death in 1035, while returning from pilgrimage, resulted in a politically troubled situation. William was a minor quite incapable of ruling Normandy by himself, and his chances of surviving as duke until his majority seemed slim. Under the protection of his feudal lord, King Henry I of France, and his aunt's stepson, Count Baldwin V of Flanders, who was also the French king's brother-in-law, William survived the murder of three of his guardians, and the first 12 years of his rule were characterised by almost constant anarchy. Nevertheless, William's long apprenticeship at the seat of power was to serve him well. In 1047, commanding his own army for the first time and supported by Henry I of France, he suppressed the last significant rebellion by his barons in Normandy at the battle of Val-ès-Dunes. Thereafter, he was dominant in Normandy (**colour plate 8**).

Although the battle marked a turning point in the history of Normandy and the beginning of a phase of powerful ducal government, relatively little is known about the

17(a)   Royal Seal of William the Conqueror

details of the conflict apart from the fact that no great military leadership appears to have been displayed on either side, and that the battle consisted of isolated conflicts between detached forces of cavalry. The revolt was led by Nigel, Viscount from the Cotentin, and Ranolf, Viscount of Basin. They were joined by lords from lower Normandy and in particular by a group of magnates from the district of the Cinglais, situated between Caen and Falaise. It was a formidable rebellion and threatened the very identity of Normandy. The Conqueror's biographer, William of Jumièges, reported briefly that 'the King and the Duke, unafraid of the strength of their enemies, offered them battle, and after many engagements between groups of cavalry inflicted a great slaughter on their foes who, at last, were seized with panic and took refuge in flight, throwing themselves into the waters of the Orne'. The twelfth-century Norman poet, Wace, reflecting on the scale of the massacre wrote 'the mills of Borbillon were stopped with dead bodies.'

17(b)   Silver penny of William the Conqueror

The defeat of the western barons at Val-ès-Dunes proved to be a decisive event in the career of Duke William. In October 1047, an ecclesiastical council met outside Caen attended by William and most of the chief prelates of Normandy. At this meeting the Truce of God, a Carolingian military convention which had not previously been adopted in Normandy, was formally proclaimed in the duchy; those present swore to observe it, taking their oaths on holy relics, including those of St Ouen which had been brought from Rouen for the purpose. Under the terms of the truce, private war was prohibited from Wednesday evening until Monday morning and during the seasons of Advent, Lent, Easter and Pentecost. These conventions were already observed in many other regions of France. Significantly, however, in the terms agreed at Caen the French king and the Norman duke were permitted to wage war between the permitted periods and were allowed to maintain forces to enable them to do so in the public interest. The truce was one of the circumstances which enabled William to become all-powerful and to impose the *pax ducis*, which in due course was established in all the areas under his control.

In the following year (1048), William joined King Henry in a successful campaign against Geoffrey Martel of Anjou who had invaded Maine. With this evidence of his military capacity and his ability to control his duchy he was accepted by Count Baldwin as a worthy husband for his daughter, Matilda, but Pope Leo IX forbade the marriage and excommunicated the couple. The formal reason for the papal ban was that the couple were too closely related, but this appears to have been a pretext and the real reason for papal disapproval is not clear. Papal opposition to the marriage was only lifted in 1059 after William had agreed to build the two great abbeys in Caen as penance, but, by that time, King Henry of France had withdrawn his support for William. Henry made an alliance with his former enemy Geoffrey Martel in an effort to recover Normandy and to destroy its precocious and powerful Duke. The armies of the new alliance invaded the duchy in 1053 and again in 1058, only to be defeated by William and to be driven out after the battles of Arques, Mortemer and Varaville (**colour plate 9**).

Following these victories, William embarked on a series of successful and reputedly brutal campaigns which eventually brought the whole of Maine under Norman control, and as a result of which he was able to add the Count of Maine to his titles. He was also able to subdue Brittany, over which he claimed lordship. The Anglo-Saxon Chronicle portrayed William as wise, powerful and 'gentle to the good man who loved God', but 'stern beyond all measure to those people who resisted his will'. During the 1050s he consolidated his control and developed military and political skills which he was later to apply with great success in England. Although, regrettably, the details are only sketchily recorded in the early part of this period, a strengthening of the feudal structure was accompanied by a general tightening up of ducal administration, most notably in the area of military service, providing the Norman duke with one of the strongest armies in Europe. Castles became a particularly important element in William's military strategy — he established them in troubled border areas and in other strategic locations, insisting on exercising his right to garrison the castles of his strongest barons. Thus by 1066 William had established himself as master of north-west Gaul, a powerful European sovereign in all but name. In 1066 William enjoyed an unparalleled position of strength in Normandy. In the words of the eminent Norman historian D.C. Douglas:

> During the decades preceding the Conquest of England, the aristocratic and ecclesiastic development of Normandy had been merged under the rule of Duke William II into a single political achievement. It might, perhaps, be summarised by saying that in 1065 a man could go from end to end of the duchy without ever passing outside the jurisdiction, secular or ecclesiastical, of a small group of inter-related families with the duke at their head.

On the eve of the events of 1066, not only was William pre-eminent in Normandy but he had successfully quelled potential opposition outside Normandy's boundaries. He had annexed Maine and Anjou, his authority was recognised in Brittany, and France — having been earlier defeated by William — was under the control of relatively weak kings. The provinces to the south-west and the west of Normandy were quiescent, and Flanders to the north had become allied with Normandy through William's marriage to Matilda. In the context of the volatile military politics of contemporary north-west medieval Europe, such circumstances favourable to William could not have been expected to prevail for very long. William took full advantage of the situation of which he was in no small part the architect and, when the opportunity arose, he seized the throne of England. It seems probable that only a ruler with the energy, ambition and administrative ability of William's status could have managed to conquer England. Undoubtedly his ability to neutralise opposition and mobilise the potential both of Normandy and its neighbours in the invasion of England were of critical importance in the story of his success.

1066 in Normandy

On hearing of Harold's accession to the English throne William sent a formal protest to England and declared his intention to invade and claim the crown that he believed had been promised him. The Norman duke then sent a mission to seek the support of Rome and, although there were some in the papal *curia* who saw the invasion as unjustified, the arguments of the great reforming archdeacon Hildebrand (later Pope Gregory VII, 1073–85) and of Pope Alexander II, a Norman sympathiser, prevailed. The Pope saw the

18   Rustic carving of Norman cavalrymen, St George's Abbey, Boscherville

pious duke as someone who could be relied upon to support religious reform and return England and its clergy, whom he regarded as schismatic, to the fold of the Church of Rome. The Pope endorsed the invasion and sent a blessed banner to Normandy. Contemporary chroniclers condemned the English church in several respects. For example, Orderic Vitalis, writing later, claimed that there had been no strict monastic discipline in England and that monks differed little from scholars in their lifestyle. Among the charges he levelled against the pre-Conquest monks was that they did not wear habits and took no vows; also, that they indulged in feasting and were able to hold property. Similarly, William of Malmesbury castigated the ignorance and loose-living of the English clergy in general. Papal approval was a valuable weapon which strengthened William's propaganda and helped guarantee the support of other princes, many of whom hoped that the 'English Crusade' would preoccupy the dangerous duke and even satisfy his apparently endless territorial ambitions.

William's designs on the English throne involved an immense amount of political and strategic planning. It was necessary for him to leave a substantial army to defend Normandy during his absence. The proposed campaign was not universally popular with his barons and they needed considerable persuasion to enter into an overseas campaign whose outcome was far from certain. Furthermore, the duchy did not actually have the manpower to provide a second army for the invasion of England. Thus, William's envoys not only bargained for mercenaries in the rest of France, they were obliged to coax the reticent Norman barons with promises of land, money and wealthy English brides. Slowly they were persuaded, and throughout the spring the Norman nucleus of William's army mustered. Transports were assembled in the ports, boats were requisitioned and new ships were built. Mercenary soldiers arrived, not only from those provinces where Normandy had a strong political influence such as Brittany and Maine, but also from Poitou, Anjou, Aquitaine, Flanders and even as far away as Aragon and the Norman settlements in southern Italy. A few of the French contingents were led by great feudal barons like Eustace of Boulogne, but the majority of mercenaries were landless adventurers who left little behind them and who, like many of the Normans, risked their lives in return for the potential spoils of victory; thus, the attack on England was to be a truly 'Norman' venture (**18**).

3 The Conquest of England

England and continental Europe

The impression is often given that Anglo-Saxon England was remote both politically and culturally from the continental mainland of Europe, and that the Norman Conquest of England represented the first significant contact between England and mainland Europe for many centuries. This is clearly untrue and William's conquest of England has to be seen within the context of long-standing and sustained links between England and continental Europe. Indeed, during the first part of the eleventh century England was politically closer to Europe than at any time since the Roman era. Viking activity had been an important feature of English life from the late eighth century onwards. Scandinavian involvement in England evolved to the point where there were four Danish kings of the recently united English kingdom in the eleventh century and for a while, under King Cnut, England and Denmark were ruled as one kingdom. The extent to which the English were associated with the Scandinavian world can be gauged from their literature; *Beowulf* is a Saxon poem about a Scandinavian hero. It is also said that Edward the Confessor, the least Danish of Anglo-Saxon monarchs, used to tell old Norse tales, and at Easter every year used to recount the story of Olaf, the 'greatest of all kings', to his bodyguard.

Anglo-Saxon involvement in continental European affairs is often poorly documented, but as early as the middle of the tenth century there was Saxon military activity in France. Æthelstan was godfather and patron to the exiled Breton prince Alan, who recovered his inheritance from the Loire Vikings in 937. Two years later, Æthelstan sent ships to Flanders on hearing that his nephew, Louis IV, was threatening coastal areas, and Æthelstan's successor King Edmund did the same in 946. Æthelred's fourth code of c.1000, which was concerned with the collection of tolls taken in London, records traders travelling from Normandy, Flanders, West Frankia, Lotharingia and Germany. Pepper and other spices were imported from the east and paid for by sales of English wool, bringing in German silver from the Ottonian empire. Additionally, England was involved in the profitable European slave trade. Anglo-Saxon traders were able to operate in the ports of the Seine and Rhine, just as their opposite numbers were able to transact business on the Thames.

In 1054, Edward sent Bishop Ælred of Worcester to the court of Emperor Henry II. It was through such visits that the latest liturgical books and models of ecclesiastical reform were brought from the continent to England. When Emma, and later Edward the Confessor's widow Edith, required the preparation of political propaganda, they turned to the services of Flemish monks. Similarly, when Edward the Confessor granted land in England to a Norman monastery he was only following Cnut's example; Cnut to Fécamp, Edward to Mont St Michel. Significantly, perhaps, both gifts incorporated a strategic Kentish port, and it is possible that one of Edward's motives in encouraging such continental connections was to keep open the question of who was to succeed him.

As far as political contacts with Normandy were concerned, at the request of Pope John XV, King Æthelred entered into a written agreement with Duke Richard I of Normandy in 991. The details of this treaty are not known, but it may have been more concerned with ecclesiastical politics in the form of the disputed succession to the Archbishopric of Rheims than issues of mutual defence. Æthelred saw the main Scandinavian threat as coming from the north and west via Norse settlements in Ireland and the Isle of Man and he focused his military response there, but after the millennium the south and south-east began to seem more vulnerable. It may have been this perception which lay behind Æthelred's initiative in seeking a closer alliance with Duke Richard II, whose sister Emma he married in 1002 (**19**). It was soon after this, according to William of Jumièges, that Æthelred sent ships to attack Scandinavian raiders based in the Cotentin peninsula, apparently without the consent of the Norman duke.

England in the eleventh century

The politics of the newly united Kingdom of England in the eleventh century were immensely complicated. There were two particularly important themes; firstly, the domination by Scandinavians of the English throne, together with extensive continued Scandinavian military activity in England, and, secondly, the inexorable process by which English and Norman politics became increasingly inter-linked as the century progressed.

Early in the eleventh century there were two major Viking invasions of England. A great fleet, led by a certain Tostig, arrived at Sandwich in July 1006, causing disruption wherever it went including the Isle of Wight, which it used as a base for further operations in Wessex in the winter of 1006–7. Æthelred sued for peace and paid £36,000 to the Viking army in 1007, whereupon it agreed to return whence it came. Two years later a large Danish raiding party led by Thorkell 'The Tall' arrived at Sandwich and proceeded to plunder in southern England. The campaign culminated with the siege of Canterbury in 1011, and led to the capture of Archbishop Ælfheah and to his eventual martyrdom at Greenwich on 19 April 1012. Subsequently a payment of £48,000 was made over to the Viking army, after which it once again dispersed. Thorkell went on to serve Æthelred, but in 1015 supported the invasion of Cnut who created him earl of East Anglia. In 1019, when Cnut was out of the country, Thorkell acted as his regent.

The Danish king Sven Forkbeard again brought his fleet to Sandwich in the summer of 1013 and moved northwards into the Danelaw where he gathered support and, eventually, gained recognition as king, forcing Æthelred to follow his wife into temporary exile in Normandy in 1013–14. It is possible that Duke Richard of Normandy had already entered into some kind of alliance with Sven who, by 1013, had made clear his intention to conquer the whole of Æthelred's kingdom. Sven's unexpected death in February 1014 caused Richard to reconsider his alliances, and Æthelred's return to England was negotiated, notionally at least, through his ten-year-old son Edward (the Confessor).

Within two years, however, Æthelred himself was dead, and soon his eldest surviving son, King Edward Ironside, was dead too, possibly murdered on the instructions of Cnut. Cnut, another of Sven's sons, married Ælgifu, daughter of the one-time earl of Northumberland Ælfhelm, and eventually became King of England. This marriage was an

19   *The redoubtable Queen
      Emma being presented with
      her life. On the right two of
      her sons, Alfred and Cnut
      and the future King Edward
      the Confessor. From a mid-
      eleventh century manuscript*

important act of conciliation, signifying union between the Danes and the English, but, in 1017, Cnut committed bigamy by marrying Æthelred's widow, the Norman queen Emma, without repudiating his English first wife. Æthelred's two sons by Emma had returned to Normandy, and, through Emma, Cnut in a curious way confirmed Æthelred's Norman alliance. A little later Edmund Ironside's two sons threatened to intervene in the troubled situation. In 1017 they had been too young to pursue their claim to the English throne and had instead found refuge at the court of the German emperor, Henry II. It was the existence of these Anglo-Saxon 'Athelings' (kings' sons) in mainland Europe, as well as the continental dimensions of Cnut's own circumstances, that made the English kingdom the focus of much princely ambition in the first part of the eleventh century.

On the death of his brother Harold, the Danish king, in 1019, Cnut returned to claim control of Denmark and the rest of his reign spanned the two kingdoms. A permanent fleet had to be maintained out of taxation to operate an empire linked by the North Sea. Cnut spent most of his time in Denmark, but in England recruited new men to support him, notably Godwine whom he created Earl of Wessex. When Cnut died in 1035 the succession to the English throne was, to put it mildly, confused. The four contenders for the throne were Harold Harefoot, Cnut's son by his first English wife, and Halfacanute, Cnut's son by Emma, and also Emma's two sons by Æthelred, Edward and Alfred. Emma summoned her two elder sons to return from Normandy, but within weeks Alfred had been murdered and his brother Edward (the Confessor) retreated hastily to the duchy. In 1037, as the situation deteriorated, Emma herself was obliged to take refuge in Flanders, and her hopes for influencing the succession to the English throne were further confounded by the death of her nephew, the Norman duke Robert, in 1037. The dukedom passed to the young William, and thus Normandy's ability to play a significant role in English politics was severely curtailed, for the time being at least.

In 1039 Halfacanute sailed a Danish fleet to Bruges in Flanders, where a planned invasion of England was forestalled by the death of Harold Harefoot in 1040. Bowing to the inevitable, an English delegation was sent to Bruges to acknowledge Halfacanute as king. Once in England, his popularity was immediately undermined when he recreated his father's Anglo-Danish empire and imposed harsh taxes in order to pay for his fleet. In 1041, Edward's star was in the ascendant and he was once more summoned from Normandy; when Halfacanute died the following year Edward succeeded him. Thus it was that disputes between rival and often short-lived rulers, and the consequent series of exiled royals on the continent, had created complex continental interests in the English succession.

During the early part of Edward's reign these continental contacts had been strengthened, and when Edward returned to England from Normandy he brought with him a number of Norman clerics and administrators. These included Robert, abbot of Jumièges, who became bishop of London in 1044 (**colour plate 10**). In 1049 Edward made Ulf, a Norman priest in his household, bishop of Dorchester, and in 1051, when Robert of Jumièges became Archbishop of Canterbury, another of Edward's priests, William, took his place in London. He also invited a group of Norman lords who were given estates in the Welsh Marches and in other strategically important locations in the country. Several of these lords constructed private castles which were more or less unknown in England at that time.

Edward the Confessor had married Godwine's daughter Edith in 1051, but, apparently encouraged by the Normans, he alienated his father-in-law and forced a showdown between them. In response, Godwine instigated a rather half-hearted rebellion against the king which failed, and as a consequence he and his family, including Queen Edith, were forced to seek exile in Flanders. The links between the Godwines and Flanders were strengthened when Tostig, son of Godwine and Harold's half-brother, married the daughter of the count of Flanders c.1051. The following year the Earl of Wessex was better prepared and was able to secure firm support in England. He returned in force, and this time it was the Normans that fled and Edward was perforce reconciled to his childless wife. Those Normans who left included Archbishop Robert. His premature departure from the primacy of Canterbury created a *cause célèbre* because Edward's choice for his successor as Archbishop, Stigand, was consistently portrayed as a usurper to the position by the Normans and was excommunicated by a series of popes. Bishop Ulf also left, but bishop William of London retained his position until his death. Meanwhile Eustace, Count of Boulogne, visited England in 1051 and married Edward's widowed sister Godgifu. Such a link with Eustace would have helped protect the English Channel and the south coast from Scandinavian fleets, but Edward was not the only one to seek a cross-channel alliance. Duke William reputedly visited England in 1051 at a time of considerable political uncertainty, although the evidence for this event is flimsy.

In 1052 Edward was obliged to recall Earl Godwine to favour, but the succession remained a pressing issue. Although there were princely pretenders immediately across the Channel, Edward's thoughts turned to his long-lost kinsman who had sought refuge in the German Empire over 30 years before. He was, however, unsure of the exact whereabouts of the Atheling Edward, son of Edmund Ironside, and his children. Bishop Ælred was sent to Cologne in search of them and, in 1057, the family returned to England from Eastern Europe, but the Atheling died soon afterwards, before he could reap any political rewards. His daughter Margaret stayed at King Edward's court until 1057 when she moved to Scotland and married the king of the Scots. Meanwhile the Atheling's son Edgar, who was a minor, was officially named 'Atheling' by Edward. Unlike his father, however, Edgar the Atheling was not a king's son, although he was to play a significant walk-on role in English politics for several decades thereafter.

William and the English throne

Apart from the disputed promise concerning his successor said to have been made by Edward the Confessor c.1051, William's claim to the throne of England lay principally through his grandfather's sister, Emma, who had been married to two consecutive kings of England, Æthelred and Cnut. Emma, sister to Duke Richard II (966–1026) and mother of Edward the Confessor, played an important part in bringing Normans and Norman customs into the English court. Immediately after he became king, Cnut married Æthelred's widow, and she subsequently gave birth to his legitimate heir to the Scandinavian Empire, Halfacanute. She was also the mother of Halfacanute's successor, Edward the Confessor. Emma could not, of course, transmit any claim to the English throne, but she was a personage of considerable political significance in English politics from the time of her first marriage in 1002 until her death in 1051. She was a formidable old lady by the time her first son, Edward the Confessor, was obliged to go to Winchester to seize her property on the pretext that her amassed wealth and power presented a threat to him. She was, curiously, supporting the claim of Magnus of Norway to the English throne, in preference to her own son. Subsequently she was effectively confined to Winchester where she died. Her headstrong individuality makes it difficult to believe that she either advocated Norman interests in England or tactfully justified English policies in Normandy, but nevertheless she reflected the fact that English kings of the eleventh century had realised they were obliged to take Normandy into account.

Edward had spent half his life in exile in Normandy, during the first years of his reign he relied on the political and military advice of his Norman comrades, and throughout his life he maintained close personal contacts with the duchy. It is possible, although unlikely, that the French chronicler's account that Edward the Confessor had named William as his successor in the early 1050s was correct. According to Norman accounts, Harold Godwinson's journey to Normandy in 1064, which is depicted in detail on the Bayeux Tapestry, was undertaken in order to confirm this recognition. Harold was shipwrecked on the coast to the north of Normandy and handed to Duke William by Count Guy of Ponthieu in one of a series of events that, on the Tapestry, ties Harold to William as his bondsman. The claim that Edward had sent Harold to promise William the succession seems contradicted by the admission by French chroniclers that Harold's presence in

20   Death of Edward the Confessor from a twelfth-century manuscript

Normandy was an accident. It is much more likely that, realising William had designs on the English throne, Harold conceived a bid of his own. It is probable that Harold's succession had been agreed even before Edward's death; indeed, such was the speed of his election that it could hardly have been otherwise. Edward the Confessor died on 5 January 1066 and on his deathbed acknowledged Harold as his successor (**20**). At dawn on the next day he was buried in his newly-built abbey at Westminster, which had been consecrated only some eight days before (**colour plate 11**). By the end of that same morning Harold had been elected by the Witan and enthroned at High Mass in the Abbey. On hearing of Edward's death and Harold's accession, Duke William of Normandy instigated the diplomatic and military preparations necessary for the invasion of England.

Since the English monarchy was elective, the promises of a previous king amounted at best to grounds of being considered as a candidate. By blood, the best candidate was the 12-year-old Edgar the Atheling, the heir apparent, Edward the Confessor's great nephew who had been brought to England by his father in 1057. However, the Witan tended to elect the most powerful candidate, the man most likely to hold the kingdom together who was, in this case, Harold. Once the Witan had elected Harold he became the rightful king of England. In Europe, however, where William had been promoting the justice of his own cause, the niceties of English tradition were unknown and Harold's case went unheard.

As we have seen, there were a number of other powerful candidates seeking the throne in addition to William who saw themselves as Edward's rightful successor. It is possible that the speed of Harold's election reflected his belief that he would soon be called upon to defend the kingdom. Cnut's nephew, King Sven of Denmark, claimed that the succession had been promised to him when Edward had been chosen in his place. King Harold Hadrada of Norway, whose army was already assembled for an invasion of England, claimed that the childless Halfacanute had promised the throne to his predecessor, King Magnus, thus giving him a legitimate claim. Also, Harold Godwinson's half-brother Tostig, who had quarrelled with the king and Earl Harold, had fled to the continent before Edward's death and had raised an army in Flanders in order to support his own claim.

The Bayeux Tapestry

One of the principal documents relating to the conquest of England is the Bayeux Tapestry. In a series of pictures, captioned in Latin, the unknown designer(s) recounts, in cartoon style, the rivalry of Harold Godwinson, Earl of Wessex, and William, Duke of Normandy, for the throne of England. The upper and lower borders of the Tapestry are inscribed with figures of birds and beasts, themes from fables and, occasionally, sly comments on the main narrative story. Although called a tapestry the work is, in fact, an embroidery, executed in coloured woollen threads on a broad ribbon of linen about 230ft long and 20in wide (**colour plate 13**). It is the only large-scale example of needlework surviving from the Middle Ages, and the almost complete survival of the Tapestry with its intricate detail has meant that generations of scholars have scrutinised its detail. Buildings and trees help frame individual episodes, which include scenes of banqueting, ships at sea, cavalry fighting at Hastings, royal and ducal palaces, churches, domestic buildings and various incidents of everyday life. Some 1500 figures of men and women, horses, miscellaneous birds and beasts, ships and buildings appear in the Tapestry (**colour plate 14**). Scenes from Aesop's fables and other images scattered throughout the borders reflect themes appropriate to the action in the main panels. The consistency of the design throughout strongly suggests a single designer, although many hands were involved in its creation. Although there is no absolute evidence, it is generally believed that this enormous work was almost certainly designed by a man and the needleworkers were both men and women.

The story recounted on the Tapestry begins when Edward the Confessor sends Harold on an unspecified mission across the English Channel. The sea crossing ends when, upon landing on the continent, Harold was captured by Guy of Ponthieu. Duke William of Normandy pays the ransom, rescues Harold and brings him to the ducal palace at Rouen, from whence the two men leave for a campaign in the Breton Marches. The Tapestry shows Norman and English troops at Mont St Michel, and then together attacking Breton castles at Rennes, Nantes and Dol (**21a** and **b**). At the conclusion of the campaign, William rewards Harold with a suit of armour and, in a particularly significant episode, Harold swears on holy relics that William will succeed Edward the Confessor when he dies (**22**). Harold returns to England, reports the story of his journey, and, when Edward dies, breaks his oath and seizes the English throne (**23**). However, just before he dies Edward appears to repudiate his promise to William and recognise Harold as his successor. In response,

21(a)   Duke William and Earl Harold joined forces to attack Conan at the castle at Dol in the Breton marches

William gathers a fleet, crosses to England and defeats Harold at the battle of Hastings. Harold dies, apparently killed by an arrow through the eye towards the end of the battle. It seems likely that the original Tapestry was longer and would have ended with the depiction of William's triumphal entry into London and his coronation at the end of 1066.

There has been considerable debate on the date and provenance of the Tapestry, but the general consensus is that it was completed within 25 years of the Conquest, probably by 1077 when the new cathedral at Bayeux was consecrated. There is circumstantial evidence to suggest that the patron of the Tapestry was William's half-brother, Odo, Bishop of Bayeux, who held extensive estates in Kent and who, with a number of his tenants, features on several occasions in the Tapestry. It is widely believed on stylistic grounds that the Tapestry was executed at St Augustine's abbey at Canterbury; Odo held extensive estates in Kent, which reinforces Canterbury's claim to be the place from where the Tapestry originated.

The invasion of 1066

Following the receipt of the news of Harold's accession to the English throne William set about preparing an invasion force (**24**). The fleet and army had originally assembled in the port of Dives-Sur-Mer, conveniently located at the mouth of the River Orne, close to Caen, for the Normans of Lower Normandy. Harold expected the arrival of the Norman fleet from this vicinity and, in anticipation of an invasion, kept the English near to the Isle of Wight from May to September. William's fleet was ready to sail by August if not earlier, but, according to all accounts, contrary winds confined it to port for a month. It appears that Harold's defences, both at sea and on the south coast, dissuaded William from sailing

21(b)   Although all traces of the castle at Dol, depicted on the Bayeux Tapestry, have disappeared, there is a rare example of a Romanesque secular arcade surviving in the town

22   *Harold swearing oath of allegiance to Duke William on holy relics — Bayeux Tapestry*

for Southampton and Winchester as the Confessor had done in 1051. When the fleet eventually did set off it sailed slowly northwards up the Norman coast, gathering contingents of men and ships from Upper Normandy to swell its numbers. According to one account the Norman fleet was blown northwards, but another tells of William stopping off for some time at his ducal palace at Fécamp before moving on to the mouth of the river Somme. Somehow the great army was kept together, and the advance to St Valéry-sur-Somme (outside the duchy) (**colour plate 12**) in August and September at least created the illusion of activity and eased the problem of supplies which could be obtained from new sources along the route of the armada.

During July King Harold assembled the Essex *fyrd* along the coast and stationed himself and his fleet on the Isle of Wight, ready to intercept the raiders at sea. The *fyrd* was a local military force in which, theoretically, all free men in Saxon England were obliged to serve. *Fyrds* rarely fought beyond the borders of the shires in which they were raised. Harold and his men were obliged to wait throughout August while the army's supplies diminished and his ships became progressively less seaworthy through the need for constant patrolling in heavy weather. Eventually on 8 September, when the wind had still not changed and the summer appeared to be over, Harold dismissed his soldiers in the south in order that they

23   Harold being crowned king by Archbishop Stigand on the Bayeux Tapestry. This scene is followed by a sighting of Halley's comet, interpreted as a bad omen

could bring in their harvests, sent his fleet to the Thames for a refit, and returned with his housecarls to London. Meanwhile Harold faced the threat of another impending invasion, this time from the north where Norway presented as great a threat to him as Normandy. King Harald Hadrada, who until a treaty of 1064 had regularly ravaged the north of Denmark and as a young man had led the Byzantine empress's Varangian Guard on campaigns in Italy, Sicily, North Africa and the Holy Land, had assembled a fleet of some 300 Viking long ships. Yet King Harold concentrated his own energies in the south, leaving the northern earls Edwin and Morcar to deal with the danger from the Scandinavians. He had been in the capital for barely more than a week when he heard that Harald Hadrada had been joined by King Harold's brother, Tostig, off the coast of Scotland, had landed in the Humber estuary, and was advancing towards York. Harold hurriedly assembled an army from around London and marched north, but was too late to join forces with Edwin and Morcar whose army was heavily defeated by the Scandinavians at Gate Fulford on 20 September. He did arrive sooner than the Norwegians had expected, however, and surprised them on 25 September at Stamford Bridge. The Battle of Stamford Bridge was an overwhelming English triumph where Harald Hadrada, Tostig and virtually all of their soldiers were slaughtered. According to one source, after the truce which formally ended the battle there were only enough Norwegian survivors to man 24 of their original long ships for the journey home.

There is one source at least to suggest that Harold had used mounted troops and archers at Stamford Bridge both for advance and pursuit. According to the *Heinskringla* (the lives of the Norse kings) the English rode upon them from all sides and threw spears and shot at them. Another account speaks of the battle ending when Harald Sigurdson was killed by an arrow which hit him in the throat. So why, if the English cavalry had indeed been so effective at Stamford Bridge, were they not used at Hastings? The answer probably lies in Harold's haste to move south and confront William.

24   *The ruined Norman palace of Lillebonne, from a nineteenth-century print. The palace, now destroyed, was the place where the Norman court decided upon the invasion of England*

Hearing the news of Harold's troubles in the north, and taking advantage of a change in the wind at last, William sailed for England. On 28 September the Norman army landed unopposed at the Saxon shore fort at Pevensey in Sussex. The fort, which was originally built by the Romans in the fourth century to fend off Saxon pirate attacks, enclosed an area of some 3ha and at that stage lay much closer to the coast than it does today (**25**). On landing William reinforced the surviving Roman fortifications. After the landing at Pevensey William was still uncertain of the situation and needed to maintain close contact with his fleet and so, on 29 September, he moved eastwards to Hastings where there was a good harbour. William built a castle, which appears as being under construction in the Bayeux Tapestry (**26**). While in Hastings, William's army plundered the surrounding countryside in order to support itself and, at the same time, intimidate the English. Evidence of this harassment appears in scenes from the Bayeux Tapestry, just before the depiction of the Battle of Hastings. In one Norman soldiers are shown setting fire to a house from which a mother and her child are escaping, while in another Normans are shown foraging for supplies (see **colour plate 13**).

Despite their overwhelming victory at Stamford Bridge, King Harold and his army had suffered great losses in the battle, sapping their strength on the eve of the Norman invasion. The traditional story told is that Harold, seated at the formal banquet in York celebrating victory over the Scandinavians, was brought, post-haste, a message to say that William had landed at Pevensey. On hearing of this second invasion he gathered what forces he could muster and marched south in one of the best-known forced marches in history, arriving in London between the seventh and eleventh of October. Harold and his troops had marched for more than 250 miles, an astonishing feat even for mounted troops

25   *The ruins of Pevensey castle from an eighteenth-century print. It was here that William's invasion force landed in September 1066*

but, fatally for Harold, impossible for his foot soldiers. These probably included his archers who, although mostly poor, normally provided their own weapons but were unable to afford horses or ponies necessary for such a forced march, and who were left behind. Also left behind were the earls Edwin and Morcar whose task it was to raise another northern army to fight the Normans.

After pausing in London for only five days, allowing him the minimum of time required to assemble more soldiers, Harold set out for the south coast. Although he was advised to wait until the arrival of the northern and western *fyrds*, Harold was determined to attack the Normans at the earliest opportunity. On the evening of 13 October he established a position on a rise known as Senlac Hill (later called Battle). The armies were roughly equal in numbers, each with about 7000 soldiers. Their armour was almost identical, but their weapons and methods were different. The Saxons fought on foot with axes and javelins, whilst the Normans, whose short, round, Latin haircuts had led to a rumour being spread that William had landed with an army of monks, were able to employ cavalry, infantry and archers.

The Battle of Hastings

During the night of 13 October, William moved his troops into position at the base of the hill on which Harold and his troops had camped. Harold had intended to deliver a surprise attack on the Normans, but William's move forced him to adopt a defensive position with his army lined up along a half-mile front on the high ground in order that the Saxons' traditional 'shield wall' effect would face the Normans if they attacked. The English had dismounted and were packed behind this wall of shields, their great Danish battle-axes drawn and ready to fight in the traditional way.

26   *The building of Hastings castle overseen by Duke William holding his Papal Standard on the left, as depicted on the Bayeux Tapestry*

William had lined up his troops in three major divisions with archers and crossbow men at the front, heavily armed foot soldiers behind them supported by armoured knights on battle horses. This strategy created mobility and full freedom of movement and, with a predominance of active, mobile archers, William enjoyed a clear advantage over Harold. If William and his army needed any further motivation it was simply that of having to conquer or die where they stood. It was William, not Harold, who was fighting on foreign soil, effectively cut off from his supply lines – it was victory or oblivion.

In the centre of the army, William commanded the Normans with the French and Flemish on his right and the Bretons on his left. At about nine in the morning he ordered his archers forward, and when they failed to make any impact on the housecarls' shields he ordered his infantry to advance. On his left the Bretons were attacked by a barrage of javelins, at which they broke and retreated down the hill, colliding with their archers and cavalry who became bogged down in the marsh. Before the Bretons could recover from their confusion some of the ranks on the English right followed them down the hill. Seeing their flank threatened the rest of William's infantry retreated. With his brother Odo and Count Eustace, William rode out to rally the centre and right. When these elements had regrouped, William detached some of his Norman knights who charged across to the left and inflicted heavy casualties on the English contingent that had been attacking the Bretons. Then, with his flank regained, William advanced his cavalry. His knights reached the English line and remained ineffectually engaged with a wall of shields for some time, but eventually the Normans in the centre began to fall back slowly. Again some of the English ranks gave chase and again they were severely punished by a cavalry charge to their flank. After the battle the Normans claimed that these withdrawals had been intentional and, although some modern historians have questioned this claim, 'feigned retreat' was a regular Breton and Norman tactic. The Bretons had used it many times in the previous two centuries, and the Normans had adopted the tactic and used it effectively themselves on several occasions, most recently at the battle of Arques in 1053 (see **colour plate 9**).

The casualties suffered in the defeat of their counter attacks so reduced the English numbers that they were forced to shorten their line. At either end there was now a gap of solid ground between their flank and the marsh. In a late bid for victory before nightfall, William ordered his entire army to advance. Harold's army crumbled from each end towards the centre until Norman knights broke through to the housecarls, and the king, who may already have been wounded in the eye (according to the Bayeux Tapestry), was cut down behind his standard (**27, colour plate 14**). The remnants of the defeated *fyrd* fled with the victorious Normans in pursuit; yet it was the pursuers who were to suffer a serious setback late in the day, when many Norman knights were killed in a deep ditch known as the Malfosse. Norman chroniclers commented with pride that some of the most famous Norman fighters of their day died at Hastings, but it was the English who had lost their king and most of their leading nobility. One authority has claimed that the Battle of Hastings was a 'conflict between the military methods of the seventh century and those of the eleventh century'. In effect, it was the most important, yet final, act in the death of the Anglo-Scandinavian military tradition.

After the battle William expected that the surviving English aristocracy would submit to him. When no word was received from the surviving English leaders after five days he marched north-east along the coast, attacking and garrisoning ports on the way in order to secure his communications across the channel. After taking Dover, where he was joined by Norman reinforcements from across the Channel, he marched inland to the episcopal city of Canterbury. As they went, the Norman forces plundered the land destroying villages and farms. No direct account of the havoc the Normans caused has survived, but Domesday Book (1086) records numerous manors in southern England whose value had been reduced, presumably as a result of the passage of William's armies and their raiding parties (**28a** and **b**). William and his army appear to have been delayed on their progress northwards by an outbreak of dysentery, but after they recovered they proceeded to Southwark on the Thames to the south of London Bridge. Here a curious incident took place in the form of a skirmish between the Normans and Londoners led by Edgar the Atheling, one of the few surviving English pretenders to the throne. Clearly William did not feel capable of taking London at that stage and, having set fire to Southwark, he moved westwards down the Thames Valley in an effort to isolate the capital. As he travelled he began to receive submissions from the Anglo-Saxons, now convinced that the duke would become the next English king. Edward the Confessor's widow Edith conceded Winchester and the treasury of England at an early stage, while Archbishop Stigand travelled to Wallingford from London to transfer his allegiance to William. William then turned east along the foot of the Chilterns and eventually encamped to the north of London at Berkhampstead.

27   *The site of the high altar at Battle Abbey, reputedly the place where Harold died*

Isolated, defenceless and threatened with famine by the systematic devastation that accompanied William's circuitous march, London surrendered. While at Berkhampstead, William was met by 'Archbishop Aldred and the Atheling, Edgar and Earl Edwin and Earl Morcar, and all the chief men of London. And they submitted after most damage had been done . . . and they gave hostages, and he promised that he would be a gracious liege lord.' Eventually, on Christmas Day, 1066, William's coronation took place in Westminster Abbey, accompanied by riots in the streets of London; the 'year of the three kings' came to an end with the ultimate Norman triumph.

The consolidation of Norman control

After his coronation William began the task of restoring order to those parts of the kingdom that he had conquered. Further pillage was forbidden and the citizens of London were given a charter confirming their privileges; William promised to exact only tolerable ransoms, and offered a pardon to all those Saxons who had not fought beside Harold. In response to this offer thegns from central and northern England came to make their submission at William's headquarters, now based at Barking, and among them, according to the Norman chronicler William of Poitiers, were the earls Edwin and Morcar. Contemporary accounts suggest that King William received them cordially and even suggested that Edwin should marry one his daughters. In the event the earls were confined to the royal court as captive guests, and when he returned to Normandy in the spring of 1067 they, along with Edgar the Atheling, Archbishop Stigand and several other earls, were the principal hostages to accompany him. William's subsequent journey through Normandy was in the form of a triumphal procession.

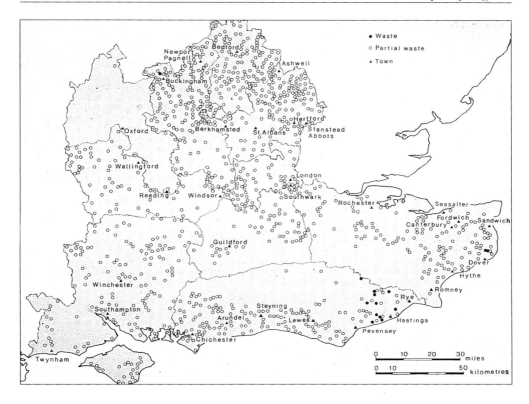

*28(a) Plan showing settlements recorded as wholly or partly devastated in 1070. 'The lines of
'Waste' Manors demark the movement of William's army, both before and after the conquest'
(Judith Dobie)*

King William sailed from Pevensey, the landing place for his invasion fleet, and went
first to the Norman capital at Rouen and then to the ducal palace and monastery of
Fécamp. This visit was marked by generous gifts to the monastery; from there he went on
to Jumièges where he attended the consecration of the new abbey church to which he had
granted Hayling Island. William also displayed great quantities of church and state treasure
from England. William of Jumièges records the astonishment of the spectators at the
richness of the gold and silver vessels and the treasures of metalwork and embroidery that
had been brought from England, and he went on to compare the English invasions of
Duke William and Julius Caesar. It was a popular theme that was to be developed by later
Norman historians. It was, perhaps, the apotheosis of William's career.

On leaving England, William had delegated the control of southern England to his half-
brother Bishop Odo, whom he created Earl of Kent, and gave power over all the country
north of the Thames to the new earl of Hereford, his old friend and compatriot William Fitz
Osbern. During William's absence these powerful governors experienced the first taste of
English resistance. There was an uprising in Hereford centred on the newly built castle
there, and the men of Kent, having found themselves an unlikely ally in Count Eustace of

28(b)   The defeated English army flees, pursued by the Norman cavalry, on the Bayeux Tapestry. At this point the Tapestry ends; originally, however, it probably continued up to the point of William's coronation at Westminster Abbey on Christmas Day 1066

Boulogne (who apparently was upset because he had not been better rewarded for his services at Hastings), besieged Dover Castle until Eustace abandoned them after the garrison's first sally. Despite these problems, by the time William returned to England at the beginning of December 1067 he had received the support of Archbishop Aldred of York. He had formed a substantial English party and saw William as the only ruler capable of maintaining order in the kingdom. Early in the following year William was able to leave the peaceful south-east and march into the furthest reaches of Wessex. Here Harold's mother and bastard sons had found refuge among those thegns loyal to the English cause who had been excluded from the Hastings campaign only by the speed of Harold's journey southward. With an army in which, for the first time, Saxon soldiers served beside his French mercenaries, William laid siege to Exeter. The city fell after 18 days, but by then Harold's family had escaped and during the next two years, posing a nuisance rather than a serious threat, his sons raided the west coast with fleets that they were able to raise in Ireland.

After the fall of Exeter, Devon and Cornwall submitted. Gloucester and Bristol followed their example, and by Whitsun William had returned to London with the south-west subdued, only to discover that there was a major uprising in the north. Three of his prime hostages had absconded; Edwin and Morcar were raising armies in Mercia, and in Northumberland a Saxon named Gospatric, to whom William had sold the northern earldom of Bernicia, was attempting to incite a rebellion in favour of Edgar the Atheling. But these uprisings were premature and half-hearted and, on William's approach, the Mercian thegns returned to their homes. By the time he reached York, Gospatric and Edgar had sought refuge at the court of the king of the Scots, Malcolm Canmore, the conqueror of Macbeth.

Despite his dominance, William was still concerned about the residual loyalty felt by the English towards their leaders and anxious not to create martyrs around whose memory rebels could rally; he therefore pardoned Edwin and Morcar. However, their room for manoeuvre was restricted by the many Norman castles that were rapidly constructed in the north with forced labour, and by the continental commanders who were granted estates in the once autonomous earldoms. After establishing a garrison and creating the foundations of a castle at York, William marched south, initiating the building of further castles on his way. The suppression of the west and north appeared to have been much easier than he could have hoped. On his return from the west he felt secure enough to bring Matilda over from Normandy and have her crowned as his Queen in Winchester. But while the uprisings of 1068 had been ineffective and ill-prepared a far more dangerous year was to follow.

The harrying of the North

The first revolts of 1069 had only limited impact, but, outraged by the indiscriminate slaughter that took place under the Norman northern commander Robert of Commines and his soldiers, the Northumbrians broke into the Norman quarters at Durham by night, murdered the soldiers in their beds, and set fire to the bishop's house, killing Robert at the same time. The men of York then rallied around a small army that had come south with Edgar the Atheling and laid siege to the castle. Again, William marched north and surprised the besiegers, upon which Edgar repeated his escape to Scotland. After ordering the construction of a second castle outside York's city walls, William returned to the south.

The most significant revolt of William's reign came later that year. The rebel leaders in north-eastern England were naturally sympathetic to the Scandinavian cause and had been negotiating secretly with King Sven of Denmark, and at the end of August, Sven made his bid for the throne of England. A fleet, reputedly said to have consisted of 240 Danish longships commanded by Sven's brother and sons, sailed up the east coast and landed on the Humber where it was joined by Edgar the Atheling, Gospatric, Earl Waltheof of Huntingdon, and a number of previously pro-Norman thegns. Eventually the English rose in formidable numbers to support the rebels. By the end of September York had been sacked and burned to the ground, many of the new northern castles had been destroyed, and the survivors of the Norman garrison were prisoners in Danish ships. In the meantime the Normans suffered another blow as Archbishop Aldred, one of William's most powerful Saxon allies in the north, had died.

The news of the insurrection inspired uprisings in the south-west; William left these to his subordinate commanders and for the third time marched north. From York the Danes and their allies withdrew to the Humber, and as William was advancing to attack them he learned that the Mercians had risen on his south-western flank. Leaving his half-brother Robert with a small army to watch the enemy on the Humber, William marched into Mercia and defeated the rebels at Stafford. On his way back to the Humber, however, he received news from Robert warning him that the Anglo-Danish army was returning to York. His attempt to reach the city before them was thwarted by another group of English rebels who destroyed the only bridge across the River Aire, delaying his progress for three weeks until he found an undefended ford. Repeating the strategy he had used against London, William marched around York devastating the region as he went, and once again he was successful. Around the isolated and unfortified ruins the farms were empty, and within them the contents of the once-rich granaries were ashes. Knowing that they could not hope to withstand a long siege, the Danish commanders withdrew the bulk of their army before it was too late and sent messengers to William to bargain for peace.

Once the remains of York had been recaptured, William was again generous in his treatment of the rebel leaders and the invaders; as they made their submission he pardoned all the English commanders, and he did not pursue Edgar who once more fled to Scotland. He even allowed the Danes to shelter their fleet on the Humber for the winter, but, recognising the continuing danger they posed, paid them to remain inactive. He was, however, after this third and most serious rising, determined that the north would not defy him again, and during most of November and December, William's soldiers set about the systematic destruction of villages and farmsteads between York and Durham, slaughtering as they went. After spending Christmas at York they administered a similar punishment to Stafford, Derby and Chester. The 'harrying of the north', as this incredibly brutal episode was termed, achieved its cruel purpose, and the northern revolts were effectively over.

Eleventh-century warfare was almost always cruel, but the tactics used by William in the suppression of the north of England were widely regarded as exceptional and beyond excuse, even for the times. Orderic Vitalis wrote:

> On many occasions I have been free to extol William according to his merits, but I dare not commend him for an act which levelled both the bad and the good in one common ruin by a consuming famine . . . I am more disposed to pity the suffering and sorrows of the wretched people than to undertake the hopeless task of screening one who is guilty of such wholesale massacre by such lying flatterers. I assert, moreover, that such barbarous homicide should not pass unpunished.

Another contemporary writer, Simeon of Durham, recorded the destruction in more detail, recalling the rotting and putrefying corpses that littered the highways of England. Pestilence followed, and Aloist of Evesham tells how refugees in the last state of destitution poured into that town. Orderic Vitalis even went so far as to suggest that William made a deathbed repentance speech — 'I treated the native inhabitants of the kingdom with unreasonable severity, truly oppressed high and low, unjustly disinherited many, and caused the death of thousands by starvation and war, especially in Yorkshire' — but it is not clear what source Orderic was using apart from his imagination, and William's recantation is not echoed by any other contemporary accounts (**29**).

The south-western uprisings were suppressed by the subordinate commanders and, on his return to Winchester at Easter, William paid off most of his mercenaries. But there was still one pocket of resistance in East Anglia which was to be remembered more for its legendary qualities than its success. At the end of 1069 when the abbacy of Peterborough on the edge of the rebellious Fen country fell vacant, William appointed the abbot of

mid him to baldepine eorle · 7 he his ealle under fengc · 7 in
þæron ealne þone pinter þær. *ætiǫede cometa xiiii kl may*
m̃ itoio · lxvi.   On þirru ǫeaue, man halǫode þer
mynhter æt peftmynftre on ealda mærre dæǫ · 7 fe cyng
eadpard forðferde on tpelfta mæffe æfen · 7 hine mann
be byriǫede on tpelftan mæffe dæǫ · innan þære nipa·
halǫodre cyrcean on peftmynhtre · 7 hapold eorl fengc
to engla lander cynerice · fpa fpa fe cyng hit him ǫe uðe·
7 eac men hine þær to ǫecuron · 7 pæf ǫebletfod to cyn
ǫe on tpelftan mærre dæǫ · 7 þy ilcan ǫeare þe he cyng
pær · he forurt mid fciphere to ǫeaner Pillme · 7 þa hpi
le cõ tofus eorl in to   humbran mid · lx· fcipũ· Ead
pine eorl cõ land fyrde · 7 draf hine ut · 7 þa butfecarlar
hine forlocan · 7 he for to fcotlande mid · xii· fnaccũ· 7 in
ne ǫe mette hapold fe norrena cyng mid · ccc· fcipũ · 7
tofus hĩ to beah · 7 in bæǫen foran in to humbran oð þer
hi coman to eoferpic · 7 heõ pið feaht morkere eorl · 7
eadpine eorl · 7 fe norrena cyng ahte fiǫef ǫe peald · 7 man
cydde hapode cyng hu hit þær þær ǫe don 7 ǫeporden ·
7 he cõ mid myclũ hepe englifcra manna · 7 ǫe mette hine
æt ftænǫ forðef brycǫe · 7 hine offloh · 7 þone eorl tofus ·
7 eallne þone hepe ahelice oferpõ · 7 þa hpile cõ pillm eorl
upp æt heftingan on fce michaelef mæffe dæǫ · 7 hapold
cõ norðan 7 hĩ pið feaht eap þan þe hif hepe come eall · 7
þær he feoll · 7 hif tpeǫen ǫe broðra Gyrð 7 leofpine · and
Pillelm þif land ǫe code · 7 cõ to peftmynftre · 7 ealdred
arceb hine to cynǫe ǫe halǫode · 7 menn ǫuldon him ǫyld.
7 ǫiflar fealdon · 7 fyðða ii heora land bohtan · 7 ða pær leo
fric abbot of buph æt þilea feorld · 7 feclode þær · 7 cõ ham.
7 þær · dæd fone þær æfter on ælpe halǫan mæffe niht ǫod

7 abbas·

Malmesbury, Turold of Fécamp, who alongside his clerical qualifications had demonstrated prowess as a soldier. At the news of his appointment, a group of local inhabitants invited the Danes to help them resist the warrior abbot. When the Danes agreed, a thegn called Hereward the Wake guided them back through the fens. But the Danes did not defend Peterborough; they stripped the abbey of its treasures and, when Turold arrived with too few knights to challenge them, they were allowed to leave peacefully with their plunder.

Abandoned by their allies and certain that they would be punished for their revolt, Hereward and his supporters took refuge in a fortified camp on the Isle of Ely and held out until, in 1071, Edwin and Morcar left William's court to join them. While recruiting an army Edwin was murdered by his own supporters, but Morcar reached Ely with a small force. The threat was enough to bring William himself to suppress it. After several bloody assaults the stronghold was taken. Morcar was captured and remained a closely-guarded prisoner for the rest of his life, but Hereward escaped and, although he seems to have remained at large, disappeared from the historical record. Hereward's subsequent fictional adventures were the stuff of legends and made him an English hero in stories and ballads that have been recounted over the succeeding centuries.

William 'the Conqueror'

William had conquered England through his own determination against what seemed to be impossible odds. Consistency and extraordinary good luck, as well as the division and incompetence of his enemies, played their part. By 1072 the only threat to his sovereignty lay beyond the northern border, where King Malcolm had persuaded Margaret to marry him and might therefore be expected to take a greater interest in the pretensions of his brother-in-law Edgar. After a pre-emptive show of strength, in which William led his army to the Firth of Forth, the two kings concluded a treaty at Abernethy on the river Tay. Malcolm received estates in northern England (for which he paid homage), gave William his eldest son Duncan as a hostage, and agreed to expel Edgar the Atheling from Scotland.

Edgar eventually made his peace with William, was pardoned, and even granted a pension. William could afford to be generous; the young Saxon pretender had never been more than a puppet in the northern uprisings, and he was too little known in the country at large to be well supported. The only man with the authority and influence to rally the English people in a united defence had fallen at Hastings. In most of England Saxons had fought for Harold because he and the brothers who were captured or killed beside him were their earls, and in Mercia and Northumbria they had fought for him because their earls were his allies. Once Harold was dead there was no focus for resistance. They might fight for the freedom of their shires out of parochial self-interest, or for a surviving thegn out of duty, but in a kingdom that the rivalry of the earls had served only to divide the English had yet to learn how to fight consistently for England.

4 England and Normandy in the twelfth century

After the Conquest

After 1072 the English were relatively passive and, during the last 15 years of his reign, William the Conqueror spent much of his time in Normandy; he was actually absent from England for nearly three consecutive years between 1077 and 1080. During the long spells of time he spent in Normandy, William left the administration of his newly-won kingdom to regents and, in particular, to Archbishop Lanfranc (**colour plate 16**). Once he had conquered England William did not continue his invasion into the rest of Britain, although he had sufficient pretext to do so as the Welsh had supported the eastern rebels, the Irish had supported Harold's sons, and the Scots had continued to raid the northern counties. The response to this provocation was measured; in the Welsh Marches the earls of Shropshire and Hereford pushed the Norman frontier into Wales at their own pace, but later, in response to Scots attacks, a campaign led by Bishop Odo reached Falkirk in 1080. But there was no systematic attempt to conquer either Wales or Scotland to begin with, and Ireland was not brought into the Anglo-Norman sphere of operations for the best part of another century.

For the remainder of William's reign his French territories were disrupted by rebellions, including one that involved his eldest son and heir Robert Curthose, and, in addition, Flanders, Anjou and France threatened his Norman borders. Thus William had little alternative, but to consolidate his gains and remain predominantly on the defensive. He could not afford to divide his military resources between these enemies and a further British offensive. The alliance with Flanders had broken down as early as 1071 and the resulting conflict had led to the death of his prized viceroy, William Fitz Osbern. Soon afterwards there was a rebellion in Maine supported by Count Fulk of Anjou, during which the Norman garrison was expelled from Le Mans, while in the west there were difficulties with Brittany until 1086 when Count Alan of Brittany married William's daughter Constance.

There was even a Norman rebellion in England. In the years immediately after the Conquest, Normans in England depended on unity and loyalty to their commander, but William's control of the country appeared to be so demanding to some barons that early in 1075 Roger of Hereford and Earl Ralph of Norfolk planned a coup while William was in Normandy. They obtained a promise of support from Denmark, and with the enticement of the English throne they persuaded the last powerful Englishman, Earl Waltheof of Huntingdon, to join them. The plot soon collapsed and Roger and Waltheof were tried for treason. On their conviction they were sentenced to the separate penalties prescribed by the laws of Normandy and England. Roger spent the rest of his life in prison while Waltheof was executed, and thus became one of the few Englishmen to be martyred by the Normans. The fate of the English rebel served as a salutary warning, and thereafter the only leading barons who dared defy William were members of his own family.

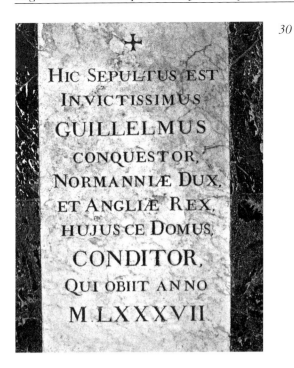

30 William the Conqueror's tombstone at St Stephens abbey church, Caen. This is a nineteenth-century replacement for the tomb, which was broken up both in the sixteenth and eighteenth centuries

King William II (Rufus) (1087–1100)

William the Conqueror died in Rouen after being fatally wounded on campaign against the French King, Philip I, at Mantes in the Norman Vexin in 1087 (**colour plate 17**). He was buried at the church of St Stephen in Caen, which had been built partly as a sepulchre and partly as penance to the Pope for his marriage and to which, after the Conquest, he had given the crown, lance and sceptre of England (**30**). On his death Normandy passed to his eldest son Robert Curthose (**31**), and England to his second surviving son, William Rufus. It is not entirely clear why the division was made, but it is probable that William was punishing his eldest son for the role he had played in uprisings in Normandy and there is a strong indication that William wished to deprive Robert of Normandy as well. However, William Rufus may not have succeeded to the throne at all if Archbishop Lanfranc had not interceded to stop Robert seizing the crown. Orderic Vitalis reported that:

> Robert was personally brave, very adventurous, a witty talker and an attractive companion, but his acts were frequently ill-considered and he was extravagant in word and deed, so that he wasted his substance and was lavish with promises upon which little reliance could be placed.

There is little doubt of Robert's charm and bravery; he conducted himself bravely during the first crusade when, it was said, neither Christian nor pagan could unhorse him. His lack of judgement was perhaps best illustrated in 1078, when he attempted to gain control

31   *The effigy of Robert Curthose, Duke of Normandy, at Gloucester Cathedral. Robert,*
William the Conqueror's eldest son, was imprisoned in England by his brother Henry I
until his death in 1134

*32   Aerial view of the northern Norman fortress town of Durham, with the great cathedral in
the centre and the castle on the right*

of Normandy by instigating a rebellion which unsuccessfully attempted to seize Rouen.
Furthermore, during Robert's time as duke much of the authority built up by his father
in Normandy was dissipated. Private castles multiplied and a confused political situation
developed. But the question remains, why did the Conqueror not disinherit Robert
altogether? Possibly because Robert had the backing of many Norman barons who had
taken an oath of loyalty to him. Normandy was not reunited with England until after the
battle of Tinchebrai (1106) where Henry I defeated Robert and the King of England again
became Duke of Normandy.

William II's accession was a signal for renewed dissent in England in support of Robert,
based largely around Norman nobles such as Roger of Shrewsbury and the Bishop of
Durham who wanted to see the Anglo-Norman territories of the Conqueror reunited. In
1088 Durham Castle (**32**) was besieged and several royal castles were captured, including one
of the strongest, Bristol, which fell to Bishop Geoffrey of Coutances and his nephew Robert

of Mowbray, Earl of Northumberland. Amongst other rebels was William the Conqueror's half-brother Odo of Bayeux, a man who had played a significant, perhaps decisive, role in the Conquest and its aftermath, but who had led a rebellion against William I in 1082 and had been reluctantly released by the Conqueror on his deathbed. He eventually surrendered outside Rochester Castle. Despite personal failings, William Rufus enjoyed a high reputation as a soldier and successfully suppressed various rebellions during his reign.

William II was involved in campaigns in Normandy in 1090–1, but in 1092 he turned his attention to western Cumberland and Westmoreland which were still under Scottish control. A castle was built at Carlisle (1092) and he began to colonise the north-west with Anglo-Norman settlers. The remainder of William II's reign was characterised by intrigue, dispute and threats of external attack. In response he consolidated Norman control in England and sent military expeditions into Scotland and Wales; both developments were accompanied by the construction of numerous castles. When Duke Robert of Normandy went on crusade in 1096 he pawned the duchy for 10,000 marks and William effectively assumed the dukedom, but soon after William's death in August 1100 Robert returned and re-established himself as duke. William Rufus, like his father, was an expansionist, and at the time of his death he was already expressing interest in acquiring territory further afield, particularly in Aquitaine. According to one account, on the day before he was killed while hunting in the New Forest, William was asked where he would spend Christmas that year and he replied 'Poitiers' — an ambition eventually realised by an English king later in the twelfth century, but not until after the Norman dynasty had been replaced by the Angevin line.

According to most accounts, William II was not a popular king: he regarded the church mainly as a source of revenue, and his strained relations with Archbishop Anselm ended in his seizure of Anselm's estates in 1097. The Anglo-Saxon Chronicle described William as being 'hated by almost all his people', and it is possible that he was actually assassinated — perhaps on the orders of his brother and successor to the throne, Henry.

Henry I (1100–35)

The youngest of William the Conqueror's sons, Henry I, succeeded his brother William Rufus to the throne. His presence at William's death in the New Forest enabled him to seize the treasury at Winchester, while his brother, Duke Robert, who might otherwise have taken the opportunity to claim England, was still on crusade. Henry was more anglicised than his two Norman predecessors. His first wife was an Anglo-Saxon princess, Matilda, who was a niece of Edgar the Atheling (his second wife was Adelaide of Louvain). Henry's rule was characterised by the strengthening of many Norman institutions, for example, the Forest Laws were probably at their most severe during his reign. Henry was also responsible for establishing a legal and fiscal framework to administer a country that had effectively been ruled by force since the Conquest. Of particular importance was the work he carried out in developing the role of the exchequer by his justiciar, Roger of Salisbury, one of a number of men of talent but lowly birth who Henry raised to authority to counterbalance the power of the barons. The Charter of Liberties (1100) promised to preserve the rights of the individual from arbitrary encroachment and the *Leges Henrici Primi* laws of Henry I provided a comprehensive record of contemporary legal custom.

There was no serious internal unrest during Henry's reign, but political troubles continued both in England and in France which he responded to with another phase of military consolidation. Henry adopted a policy of exiling potential troublemakers from England to Normandy, but this had the result of creating a potential forum for a reverse attack on England by disaffected barons, such as Robert of Bellême and William of Mortain. In 1101, Duke Robert undertook an unsuccessful invasion of England, which must have concentrated Henry's attention on the need to control, if not actually conquer, the duchy.

Shortly before Easter in 1105 Henry arrived in the Cotentin peninsula with a powerful army, intent on bringing Normandy under his direct control. Although he burned Bayeux and bribed Caen into surrender, he failed to capture the stronghold of Falaise and in August he returned home to England. He remained there for nearly a year, during which time his brother Duke Robert and Robert of Bellême visited him separately to try to negotiate peace. In July 1106, however, Henry returned to fight in Normandy, and in September he besieged William of Mortain's town of Tinchebrai. On 28 September, 1106, 40 years to the day after William the Conqueror had landed in England, an English army commanded by a Norman king fought on Norman soil against a Norman army in which the pretender to the English throne served as a commander. After little more than an hour's fighting, which was apparently not distinguished on either side, the victory at Tinchebrai was total. Normandy and England were again united. All the unlicensed castles were destroyed; land grants made since the death of William the Conqueror were cancelled and the duchy was subjected to the same ruthless fiscal administration as he had established in England. After the battle William of Mortain was blinded and imprisoned for life. Edgar the Atheling, who was a close friend of Duke Robert and had participated in the battle, was released to live in obscurity until his death in 1125. Duke Robert was sent as a prisoner to Devizes and later to Cardiff where he died in 1134 (see **31**).

After the acquisition of Normandy, Henry concentrated on the construction and refortification of defences on the coast and along the border with Scotland and Wales; important strategic castles were rebuilt in stone, and some town wall circuits, like that at Carlisle, were erected. A change in the route of cross-channel traffic which came about soon after the accession of Henry I (between Purbeck and the Cotentin peninsula) resulted in the building of major castles at Corfe, Wareham, Porchester and Carisbrooke to guard the new important coastal area.

Henry's last years were dominated by the problems of the succession following the death of his only legitimate son, Prince William, in the White Ship disaster. In 1127 Henry succeeded in extracting from the barons an oath of allegiance to his daughter, Matilda — a promise that, in the event, was not to be honoured. In 1135, while hunting in the Forest of Lyons to the south of Rouen, he was taken ill with a fever that was said to have been caused by eating lampreys which his physician had specifically forbidden. He died in his hunting lodge on 1 December. The only one of his many illegitimate children beside him was his son, Robert of Gloucester. His body was taken home to England on 4 January 1136 and was buried in the church of the great Cistercian monastery which he had founded at Reading.

The Anarchy

Henry I was succeeded by his nephew, William the Conqueror's grandson by his daughter Adela, Stephen of Blois (1135–54), Count of Mortain and Boulogne and feudal lord of half a million English acres from Lincolnshire to Kent. Stephen seized the crown with the support of the church and those Norman nobles who opposed Geoffrey's Angevin connections. But Stephen's ineffective rule soon alienated his supporters and in 1138 Robert, Earl of Gloucester, Matilda's half-brother, changed sides and started a rebellious campaign against the king. Shortly afterwards the Scots invaded England and, although defeated at the Battle of the Standard, took Northumberland, Carlisle and later, Durham. In 1139 Matilda herself invaded England and, before long, controlled most of the west.

Stephen's reign is generally known as 'the Anarchy' — 19 years of interrupted civil war between the supporters of Stephen and the supporters of Matilda. One chronicler complained that the land was filled with castles, although few of them had been built by the king. During the Anarchy, as well as the extensive construction of siege works, churches and monastic sites were fortified. The monks were ejected from the Bridlington and Coventry priories and Romsey Abbey, while ringworks were thrown up around churches at such places as Merrington (Co. Durham) and St Martin's Thetford, and a castle was built within the precincts of Reading Abbey.

Many castles that had been built by Stephen's predecessors passed from his control, either into Matilda's hands, or into those of men like Ranulf, Earl of Chester, at Lincoln. For such men the civil war presented an opportunity to consolidate their own authority in those parts of the country where they had extensive estates. Such men included Baldwin of Redvers at Exeter, Earl Miles at Gloucester and Hereford, Earl Simon at Northampton and Hugh Bigod at Norwich (**colour plate 18**). Until 1143 even the Tower of London was under the control of Geoffrey of Mandeville whose allegiance varied from year to year (**33a** and **b**). The lords, it was claimed, 'burdened the country with forced labour on their estates'. Royal control over fortification had broken down and everywhere hastily constructed or 'adulterine' castles were being thrown up.

Though no longer the master of his kingdom, Stephen was by no means an incompetent general, and, if many royal castles were lost, others were gained to take their place. In 1136, for example, he captured Exeter Castle from Baldwin de Redvers and compelled him to surrender Carisbrooke. In 1138 he took Bedford Castle from Miles of Beauchamp and Shrewsbury from William Fitz Alan. In 1139 he forced Roger, Bishop of Salisbury, and Alexander, Bishop of Lincoln, to hand over to him the castles which they had strengthened; Malmesbury, Sherborne, Devizes and Salisbury (**33**), belonging to the former, and Newark and Sleaford belonging to the latter. Only Nigel, Bishop of Ely, resisted, but Stephen, having made his way across the marshes, had little difficulty in capturing the newly fortified castle there and garrisoning it with his own knights. In 1144, nearly 80 of his workmen were killed while constructing a temporary earthen castle outside Lincoln Castle. The earthworks which he threw up in front of Corfe Castle in 1139 are known as 'Stephen's Rings', and as Sir Howard Colvin remarks these 'may not inappropriately serve as a memorial to a king who must have been something of an expert in the siting and construction of such ephemeral earthworks'.

33(a)   Vertical aerial view of the Tower of London with its several defence circuits

33(b)   The plain, heavy Norman interior of St John's chapel, Tower of London

In 1141 Stephen was captured at Lincoln and held for several months before being exchanged for the Earl of Gloucester after the defeat of Matilda's forces at Winchester, where they had attempted to besiege the royalist-held Wolvsey Palace. Stephen's victory at Farringdon in 1145 was a turning point and Matilda, her cause weakened by her own unpopularity and Gloucester's death in 1147, withdrew in 1148. The final years of Stephen's reign were relatively peaceful, but he quarrelled with the church and failed to obtain acknowledgement of his son, Eustace, as his successor. On 6 November 1153 the Treaty of Winchester brought the civil war formally to an end when Henry I's grandson, Matilda's son by Geoffrey of Anjou (**34**), Henry Plantagenet, was acknowledged as the heir to the throne. Stephen's only surviving son William, earl of Surrey, received generous compensation as part of the Treaty.

The end of Norman England?

Within a year of the Treaty of Winchester, Stephen was dead and the Norman dynasty had come to an end. Henry II (1154–89), the first of the Angevin kings, rapidly restored order in England and in Normandy, where he had already been made duke in 1150. Legal and other governmental institutions were revived and expanded into an administrative system that was to rival that of Rome and, through the acquisition of territories by marriage, diplomacy, and force of arms, the Angevin successor to the Norman throne became master of western Europe from the Cheviots to the Pyrenees.

Henry assembled a team of able administrators and introduced a number of remarkable reforms. The Assize of Clarendon (1166) established the jury system, and the introduction of Possessory Assizes and the Grant Assize contributed greatly to the centralisation of Government, forming a milestone in the development of the judicial system. Henry received the homage of Malcolm II of Scotland who returned Northumberland, Westmorland and Cumberland to England. He subdued the Welsh and obtained the submission of the Irish kings. Nevertheless, his reign was tainted by the tragic events resulting from the appointment in 1162 of his Chancellor, Thomas Becket, as Archbishop of Canterbury. Their dispute over the relative rights of church and state led to Becket's exile and subsequent murder at Canterbury, a crime of which Henry was absolved at Avranches in 1172 where he did penance for the crime. His reign was further marred by the rebellions of his quarrelsome sons in 1173–4 who, with the support of his disaffected barons and of Scotland, rebelled against their father. In 1189 he was defeated in battle by his son Richard in alliance with Philip II Augustus of France, and shortly afterwards he died at Tours.

Some historians have stressed the significance of what could be interpreted as the premature end of the Norman rule in England, but the Norman style of government survived. It perhaps seems curious to us that the Norman dynasties, both in England and in Sicily, were more concerned with the perpetuation of the family than with the purity of the Norman line. Thus, in common with other European principalities, intermarriage between ruling families was regarded as desirable. It is, perhaps, the historian looking backwards, anxious to compartmentalise dynasties, that sees breaks which were not necessarily there. It can be argued with some conviction that the Angevin Kings were essentially Norman in all but name. We only have to look briefly at the career of the

34   *Geoffrey of Anjou (Plantagenet) (d. 1151), father of Henry II whose succession to the English throne brought a large French empire with it*

second of the Angevin kings to appreciate the shift of emphasis in European affairs that had been brought about by the Norman Conquest of England. Richard I 'Coeur de Lion' (1189–99) was, and remains, a national hero, but he visited England only twice as king, once for three months and later for two. Richard's great grandfather was Henry I and Richard operated in the manner of a Norman monarch — as a crusader and as a political entrepreneur for whom national boundaries had little significance.

It seems appropriate to finish this brief political survey by observing that in 1200 the affairs of England and France were interlinked in a fashion that would have been unthinkable if the Conquest had not taken place. Ironically, in view of their origins, one of the major lasting contributions attributable to the Norman Conquest was that it largely severed the political links between England and Scandinavia that had been so much of a feature of the late Anglo-Saxon period. To underline this point, it is significant that when Richard I went on crusade he left behind him in government as regents in England William Longchamp, Bishop of Ely, and Walter of Coutances, Archbishop of Rouen.

In the twelfth century England's political and cultural relationship with the French speaking world was particularly close and yet also ambivalent. Since the Norman Conquest, England had been part of a cross-channel dominion ruled by the ducal dynasty of Normandy. The English aristocracy had been expropriated and replaced by one that saw itself as Norman or, at least, Anglo-Norman in character. Socially, England and the northern parts of France were brought closer together than they had ever been. King and nobility regarded the two parts of the realm as one and sought to bring them together again when after 1087, on the death of William, they were temporarily separated. Yet at the same time, and by a paradoxical process of development, the imposition of alien rule and the disregard shown by the Normans for the traditions and customs of the English people encouraged a gradual re-awakening of English identity. Culturally, in the twelfth century England and Normandy began to grow apart. The English found a new pride in their Anglo-Saxon past and the Normans in France drifted into the orbit of Capetian Paris. By the reign of King John the two states were forging quite separate identities. King John's loss of the duchy to the French in 1204 can be seen in this sense as merely the final stage of a process of estrangement that had begun at least half a century earlier.

By 1200 England and, to a lesser extent, Wales were enjoying a degree of prosperity and everywhere there is evidence of great energy and industry. The imprint of this intense activity is still with us today both in town and country. Without the Normans would the towns have expanded and been redesigned, would the churches, cathedrals, and monasteries have been rebuilt and would hundreds of castles have been erected? No doubt some of these events would have occurred irrespective of who was ruling. However, what does seem certain is that the Normans were different enough from the Anglo-Saxons to see themselves as 'conquerors' and colonists and acted accordingly. Many of the activities of the eleventh and twelfth centuries occurred because the Normans had the wealth, energy and ruthlessness to impose a new face on an old country. What would have happened to the Normans if they had failed at Hastings? No doubt they would have gone the same way as the other contemporary French kingdoms and duchies and been absorbed by the nascent France earlier than they eventually were. We would certainly not have had very much by which to remember them apart, perhaps, from their extraordinary architectural accomplishments in Sicily and southern Italy. The Norman Conquest of England gave the Normans an entity which they would otherwise not have enjoyed, as well as respectability.

It is a paradox that, although it was in England that the Normans achieved their greatest success in all fields, in the long run the Conquest of England turned them into Englishmen. Although, initially, the new Norman aristocracy largely despised the English and their customs, they were operating essentially within an English framework. English traditions and institutions were able to survive because Norman penetration of English society was at such an elevated level, and eventually the English absorbed their Norman masters.

The end of Normandy

Although the Norman royal dynasty in England came to an end in 1154 the kings of England were to rule over Normandy for a further 50 years, but throughout this period there were persistent problems with the French monarchy. These disputes were greatly exacerbated by quarrels over the new French territories that had come under English control with the accession of the Angevins and Henry II's marriage to Eleanor of Aquitaine in 1152. Rouen had became the administrative centre of a vast Anglo-Norman territory, extending from the Pyrenees to Hadrian's Wall. The importance of the Norman capital was recognised as throughout the twelfth century the kings of England were invested as dukes of Normandy in Rouen Cathedral after their coronation in Westminster Abbey. English interests now extended throughout the whole of western and central France and, inevitably, brought them into conflict with the French crown. Normandy, which lay adjacent to the royal lands, tended to bear the brunt of any dispute between England and France anywhere on the continent.

In 1173 there was a serious uprising against Henry, both in England and in Normandy. This involved Henry's by now estranged wife Eleanor, his young sons and King Louis VII of France, but the rising was crushed later the same year following an abortive attack on Rouen. Nevertheless, throughout his reign and that of his successor, Richard I, the English monarchs were obliged to raise heavy taxes in England to fight French wars. In the 1190s vast loads of treasure were shipped across the English Channel to supplement the rapidly diminishing revenues of Normandy. In 1196 Hubert Walter, the Archbishop of Canterbury, declared that in the previous two years alone he had provided 1,100,000 marks of silver for the king's use to fight French wars.

Richard I and King Philip Augustus of France had become enemies during the third crusade and, when Richard was being held prisoner, the French king used the opportunity to attack the Norman Vexin (the eastern marcher area of Normandy) and win the important border town of Gisors (**colour plate 19**). He then went on to lay siege to Rouen which, under the command of Robert, Earl of Leicester, successfully resisted and forced him to withdraw. Richard's brother, the future King John, was eager to take advantage of Richard's troubled situation to try to supplant him and paid homage to the French king. He agreed to marry Philip's sister Alice, and then returned to England to stir up rebellion there. Measures taken by his mother, the redoubtable Queen Eleanor, effectively contained John, but not before he had sacrificed Philip's territory both in Normandy and Touraine (1194).

On his return to England from being held prisoner in Germany in the middle of May 1194, Richard crossed the Channel with a fleet of 100 ships to engage in a long struggle which was to last until his death five years later. After recapturing lost territory in France outside Normandy, Richard started to build Château Gaillard at Les Andeley, 'his beautiful castle on the rock'. It was strategically placed in a commanding position on a bend in the river Seine, and was built under Richard's personal supervision with the most up-to-date engineering science that he had learned in the Levant. It became Richard's headquarters and his favourite residence during the remainder of his life, although it was immensely expensive. £49,000 was spent on the defence of the castle in 1197–8 alone. Fighting continued in Normandy and, during 1198 and April 1199, Richard was able to re-occupy a large part of the Norman Vexin including Gisors, which fell to him in September 1198. In the rout that followed it was recorded that, 'such was the crush at the gate of Gisors that the bridge broke under them and the king of France himself . . . drank of the river.' The fighting in which Richard lost his life was nothing to do with Normandy. It happened while besieging the castle at Chàlus to punish a baron of the Limousin over a dispute involving treasure trove; an arrow struck Richard in the shoulder. The wound proved fatal and he died on 6 April 1199.

The death of Richard was followed by a disputed accession involving his mother Eleanor and the minor, Arthur of Brittany. John acted with remarkable decisiveness and, having secured the royal treasure which was at Chinon, he went to Rouen where he was invested with the duchy of Normandy on 25 April. He continued to England where he was crowned king at Westminster on 27 May. However, the war with the French king continued and, during a truce in 1200, Philip regained the Vexin with the exception of Château Gaillard and the county of Evreux.

The French forces continued to press westwards and gradually Normandy disintegrated. In December 1203 John retreated to England for no obvious reason, by which time eastern Normandy had largely passed out of his control. Philip had driven wedges deep into various parts of the duchy. Alencon in the south and Vaudreuil, which guarded the river approach to Rouen, had been surrendered by his castellans, and the greater part of the duchy between the Eure and the Risel was also in French hands. Château Gaillard alone offered serious resistance and for six months, from September 1203 until March 1204, defended by Roger de Lacy the constable of Chester, it held up the French advance (**35**). The castle capitulated on 8 March 1204, effectively marking the end of Anglo-Norman rule in the duchy. Once the great castle on the Seine had fallen, Philip Augustus faced little opposition from the Norman barons. Falaise, Caen, Bayeux, Cherbourg and Barfleur in turn all surrendered without resistance. While Philip was securing the duchy from the east the Bretons attacked from the west, capturing Mont-St-Michel and Avranches as they advanced. There was no need to besiege Rouen, which was now completely cut off. On Midsummer Day 1204, Rouen, together with the two castle fortresses of Arques (see **colour plate 9**) in the north and Verneuil in the south, came to terms with the French king. The Channel Islands were all that was left of the Norman duchy in English hands.

Following the French Conquest, there was no formal annexation of the duchy by France and John and subsequent English kings maintained their claim to Normandy. Philip Augustus issued a general decree confiscating the lands of all Normans who were

35   Château Gaillard, Richard the Lionheart's great fortress castle overlooking the River Seine
to the east of Rouen. Its capture by the French king in 1204 initiated the collapse of Normandy

in England and who failed to return by a given date. John retaliated with a similar order affecting the estates of Normans who adhered to Philip. Those barons who held lands in both England and Normandy had to choose and sacrifice their property in one country or another, in effect, they were obliged to become either Englishmen or Frenchmen. With few exceptions, such as William Marshal, they could no longer be both. Although the French continued to recognize Normandy as a distinct province observing its Norman customs and laws, all the evidence suggests that, in the words of Ralph Davis:

> The kings of England and France had forced the barons of Normandy to choose between their two countries, no one stood up to protest that he was neither English or French, but Norman. On the contrary the English became more English and the French more French and the Normans as history had known them disappeared.

Under the Treaty of Paris in 1259, King Henry III surrendered the English claim to Normandy in return for Henry's lordship over Gascony. During the reign of Edward I and in the Hundred Years War, the English were again to occupy Normandy, along with much of the rest of western France, but by this time its political autonomy had disappeared.

5 The fabric of Anglo-Norman England

The conquest of England represented the Normans' greatest political and military triumph. After the Battle of Hastings England received a new royal dynasty, a new aristocracy, a new church, a transformed art and architecture and, in court circles at least, a new language. The Normans were supremely self-confident, arrogant and led by a devout Christian, and theirs was the first and only successful Christian conquest of England. The nature and extent of the consequences of the Norman Conquest on England and the English has been a matter of considerable and protracted debate. The results of the Norman take-over were sometimes obvious, with the erection of castle fortresses and great cathedrals which incorporated all the self-aggrandisement of colonial architecture. Other changes in, for example, language, literature and place names were, however, far more subtle in their impact.

Initial Norman instincts were to accommodate the defeated English, and during the years immediately after the Conquest William attempted to maintain the substance and form of Edward the Confessor's government and to incorporate leading Saxons within his court, the military and the church. It was not until 1070, after the series of major rebellions, that William's rule became more repressive and, in addition to military reprisals, continental feudalism was more rigorously imposed. Increasingly, the contract between king and lord land-tenure was related directly to military service. Military organisation was also brought up-to-date with trained cavalry becoming the back-bone of the army in England as in Normandy.

The changing face of Anglo-Norman England

By 1086, in the England depicted in the folios of Domesday Book (**colour plate 20**), only a handful of the 180 greater landlords or tenants-in-chief were still English and it is estimated that the new land owners replaced 4–5,000 Saxon thegns. The crown itself had acquired one-fifth of the land and much of the remainder was held by a select few of William the Conqueror's favourites, who had come with him or followed him from France and the Low Countries. The power and wealth of the country was concentrated in the hands of a small Norman elite and it has been estimated that about half the country was controlled by a group of no more than ten men, most of whom were William's relatives. As the old order was dismantled the earldoms were broken up, and in their place William established a new landed hierarchy modelled on continental feudal society. In principle all land belonged to the king; even the great barons were only tenants in chief, holding their estates in the fee of knight's service by which they were required to provide the king with varying quotas of knights for

36 *Map showing Anglo-Norman palatinates and castleries in vulnerable areas in the eleventh century*

up to 40 days in each year. With this contract William retained the right to be universal landlord and supplanted the Saxon *fyrds* with a reliable and experienced corps of cavalry.

Nevertheless the obligation was hardly onerous to the tenants in chief, most of whom could command more men than their quotas required. They were able to meet their obligations through the chain of lesser barons and knights to whom they sub-let manors in return for the same military service. In addition, they were often able to dominate the indigenous inhabitants of their new estates with permanent retinues of professional landless knights, who manned the manorial castles that became the chief legacy of the Norman occupation. A number of English thegns and freemen became tenants and paid a proportion of their agricultural produce to the Norman lord of the manor in return for part of their former freehold.

In the Welsh border palatinates the new earls of Chester, Shrewsbury and Hereford were allowed to exercise many of the royal prerogatives, but throughout the rest of the kingdom William had even more power than he held in Normandy (**36**). The king was the largest landowner in each shire and the government of the shires, which were kept in their Saxon form but which began to be called counties, was delegated to newly appointed sheriffs. The sheriffs lived on the royal estates during their tenure of office and ruled with all the authority of the viscounts in Normandy. Control over the administration of

temporal justice was restored to the crown. In the shire courts, from which the earls were excluded, the sheriffs usually sat alone without the bishops; even private manorial courts were supervised by special commissioners who investigated the conduct of all temporal courts and assessed the royal revenue in each shire.

The Norman castle

One of William's earliest tasks after the Conquest was to provide a secure political and military base in England. We have already observed that he chose the castle as the means of achieving this end. The earliest phases of the fortification between 1066 and 1071 followed a similar pattern to the early part of the Roman Conquest of Britain in the first century AD. If the horse had proved decisive at the battle of Hastings, then it was the castle that was to be the chief weapon of occupation. Castles were built along the south coast from Exeter to Dover. A scatter of fortification in the Midlands stretched up as far as Lincoln and York. There was a concentration in the West Midlands and in the Welsh Marches where Chester formed the north-western point of the attack and, at the estuary of the river Wye, Chepstow the southernmost (see **colour plate 15**). To begin with, the north-western chain of defences roughly coincided with the line of Icknield Street, which

38   The badly eroded castle motte at Cambridge

the Romans originally had intended as the north-western boundary of their occupied territory in Britain. By the early 1070s castles were being built to the north of this line, with particular concentrations in those areas of rebellion against the Normans. Castles were also rapidly constructed within all the shire capitals to act as administrative and strategic centres for the Normans. By 1086 there were at least 50 castles in England for which we have documentation, and undoubtedly there were very many more that did not feature in contemporary records (**37**).

Outside towns, castles were built to act as local and regional bases for the new Norman aristocracy in villages and in the countryside, and they featured particularly in areas of potential trouble such as the Welsh and Scottish marches. In the first instance these castles were of earth and timber and known as 'motte and baileys' (**38**). The term derives from the Norman French *motte*, meaning mound, and *bailey*, the attached enclosure. Such structures could be erected rapidly using materials to hand and, if destroyed, they could be quickly rebuilt. They provided a base for cavalry to control a region and at the same time provided safe havens for the Normans when things were going badly. Castles were perfect for the task of occupying and subduing England, and, later on, south Wales and Ireland. An early twelfth-century description of the castle at Mercham in Flanders provides a valuable record of this type of fortification, confirming recently excavated archaeological research in early castles:

> It is the custom of the nobles of that region . . . in order to defend themselves from their enemies to make a hill of earth, as high as they can, and encircle it with a ditch as broad and deep as possible. They surround the upper edge of this hill with a very strong wall of hewn logs, placing towers on the circuit,

39   The great Norman keep at Kenilworth castle, Warwickshire

according to their means. Inside this wall they plant their house (*domus*), or keep (*arcem*), which overlooks the whole thing. The entrance of this fortress is only a bridge, which rises from the counterscarp of the ditch, supported on double or even triple columns, till it reaches the upper edge of the motte (*agger*).

By the time Norman control was firmly established during the second half of the twelfth century, castles were used, not so much against the native English, but against warring factions in the Norman camp, most notably during the civil war between Stephen and Matilda. Castles of territorial warfare, the motte and baileys, were replaced by stone constructions or they were abandoned; during the twelfth century, the stone keep became increasingly common (**39**). In France, such keeps were known as *donjons* (Latin *dominium*, 'Lordship'). We do not know precisely where the stone tower keep originated, but in the tenth and eleventh centuries western European keeps may have evolved in design from Byzantine and middle-eastern defensive towers. The earliest known reference to a stone castle in France is to Doué-la-Fontaine, built by the count of Blois in about 950. Another early example was built by the count of Anjou, in the form of a two-storey hall tower at Langeais in Touraine, in about 990. Duke Richard I's fortress at Rouen, which has long since disappeared but is depicted on the Bayeux Tapestry, may have provided the model for the early great tower-keeps in England in places such as Richmond (Yorks). Conversely, the designs of the very early stone keep at Chepstow, started by William Fitz Osbern, was probably based on Norman ducal palaces (see **colour plate 15**).

Castles were very much the hallmark of the Normans and were resented by the Anglo-Saxons, who at first regarded them almost as a secret weapon, but gradually they became an essential feature of Anglo-Norman life (**40**).

40   Aerial view of Castle Rising, Norfolk, one of the great palace castles of Norman England

The King rode into all the remote parts of his kingdom and fortified strategic sites against enemy attack. For the fortifications called castles by the Normans were scarcely known in the English provinces, so the English, despite their courage and love of fighting, could put up only a weak resistance to their enemies. (Orderic Vitalis)

Norman castle boroughs

The castle borough was a peculiarly Norman development, which in Normandy enabled the creation of powerful urban centres such as Caen. In some cases topographical and archaeological evidence demonstrates that the construction of a town castle must have caused considerable disruption. Domesday Book graphically records the impact of this process, whereby already existing property had to be destroyed to make room for the castle at shire capitals such as Shrewsbury, Oxford (**41**) and Lincoln. At York, the building of the castle destroyed one of the seven wards recorded in Domesday; at Lincoln, 160 houses were destroyed, and at Shrewsbury 51 houses. Smaller-scale destruction is mentioned in 1086 in Cambridge (**38**), Canterbury, Gloucester, Huntingdon, Stanford, Wallingford and Warwick. At Wallingford, for example, the plantation of the great motte

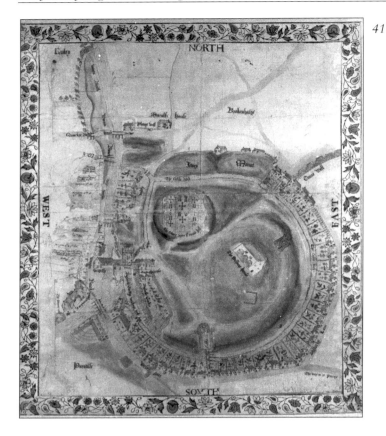

41   Sixteenth-century plan of Oxford castle showing the motte with a stone tower in the centre, with the large castle bailey around it. On the left-hand side is the Mill Stream that reinforces the defences on the south side of its castle

within a quadrant of the Saxon *burh* must have destroyed a large built-up area (see **5**). The topography of other *burhs*, such as Wareham (Dorset), Worcester, Tamworth (Staffs) and Hereford show a similar pattern, with the new castle being built either within the Saxon town or immediately adjacent to it.

Of the first 25 Norman town plantations, 18 were located alongside a castle and one of them took its name from a new castle built on the River Tyne (Newcastle). At Windsor the Saxon settlement at Old Windsor was spurned and the castle was built on a chalk promontory, which forms the only strong point in the Thames valley between London and Wallingford. New Windsor (the site of the present town) was later grafted onto the castle.

In the case of Old Sarum (Wiltshire), the Normans chose a prehistoric hillfort which now forms one of the most impressive of archaeological monuments in England (**42**). The circular mound, which formed the inner bailey of the Norman castle, sits in the centre of the earthwork surrounded by a deep and wide ditch. The original hillfort defences were deepened and heightened in order to form what was in effect the outer bailey of a concentric castle. Within the bailey the ground was levelled-up with quantities of chalk from the enlarged ditch. Bishop Osmund was allowed to build his new cathedral in the north-west segment when the see of Sherborne was transferred to Salisbury between 1075 and 1078, and the eastern limit of the cathedral precinct was defined by a bank. There appears to have been a borough here in the immediate post Conquest period, but its

42   *Aerial view of the Bishop of Salisbury's Norman castle and cathedral at Old Sarum. They are located within the reinforced defences of an Iron Age hill fort, which was abandoned in favour of 'New' Salisbury early in the thirteenth century*

precise location remains something of a mystery. Clearly, there was not room within the fortifications for a large town, but there is little trace of urbanisation adjacent to the outer defences, which would have provided the most obvious site.

At Devizes (Somerset), the relationship between castle and town is far clearer. The original name, *burgus de devisis*, indicates that the borough was sited at the divide, or boundary, between two manors, Bishop's Canning and Potterne, both owned by Bishop Roger of Salisbury. It is known that he built a castle here c.1120 which replaced an earlier one which had been destroyed in 1113. Devizes provides one of the best examples of a town plan where the castle played a dominant role in shaping the layout. The streets are aligned with the castle defences in a distinctive semi-circular shape. There are two separate market places, side by side, both curving and reflecting the shape of the castle nucleus. The outer market place is the earlier, the inner one representing later colonisation of the castle bailey (**43**).

The topography of the village of Pleshey (Essex) demonstrates similar characteristics. In 1174, William de Mandeville obtained licence from Henry II to build a castle just off the upper Chelmer valley, seven miles north-west of the future site of Chelmsford. The name of the castle, Pless, was also taken for the town that grew up within an earthen wall, which was built out in a loop from the castle forming a large second semi-circular bailey. Although no borough charter survives, thirteenth-century references to burgesses indicate that it had urban pretensions. The settlement never developed beyond its original design and today presents an obviously regular formation. Apart from Devizes and Pleshey, Richmond (Yorks), Launceston (Cornwall), Wisbech (Cambs), Totnes (Devon) (**44**), Eye (Suffolk) and Plympton (Devon) also have semi-circular street plans dictated by the shape

43   Aerial photograph of Devizes, Wiltshire, showing the castle (centre left), with the town forming a series of concentric outer baileys. To the left of the castle lay the great hunting park

of the respective castle defences. At New Buckenham (Norfolk) the town is laid out on a grid plan to the shape of a second castle bailey.

Some of these castle towns were stillborn or enjoyed a short life of only a few generations. Today they are often only stunted settlements, like Richard's Castle or Kilpeck (**45**) in Herefordshire or Caus in Shropshire. Few, if any, houses remain, and the surviving earthworks are the only indication of the line of the town walls and internal tenements. In some places, the borough occupied what amounted to little more than an outer bailey of the castle, and many of the Welsh border failed towns, such as Cefnllys, Dryslwyn, Dolforway, Huntingdon, Old Dynevor, Bere, Skenfrith and Whitecastle, show little evidence today of their former urban status (**colour plate 21**).

Planned towns

During the Middle Ages many hundreds of new to towns were created in England and Wales. Professor Beresford in his pioneer work *New Towns of the Middle Ages* (1967) showed that there was a dramatic increase in town plantation immediately after the Norman Conquest (**46**). The creation of new towns had been quite common in Normandy before the Conquest, where at least 12 bourgs had been created by 1066. William himself had planted two bourgs at Caen, close to the ducal bourg, an operation he repeated when he added the borough of Mancroft to Norwich. The term *novus burgus* is actually applied to Norwich in Domesday — the only other place where it is used is at Quatford in Shropshire. As there is no physical trace of any urbanisation here, his reference may reflect an unfulfilled ambition for the creation of a new town or, more probably, it refers to Bridgnorth, which lies a few miles upstream on the river Severn.

*44   Aerial view of Totnes, Devon, showing how the street plan of the town mirrors the castle
(centre left), before running down to the river (right)*

Another Shropshire town, Ludlow, which lies towards the eastern edge of the Welsh Marches, was one of the most successful of the medieval new towns. Since St John Hope's paper on the *Ancient Topography of the Town of Ludlow* was published in 1909, Ludlow has been recognised as a classic example of Norman town plantation. It was built by Roger de Lacy on the river Teme, on the edge of his extensive rural manor of Stanton Lacy, at the beginning of the twelfth century. The town is encircled on three sides by the Teme, and this natural defence is reinforced by a sandstone ridge that presents a precipitous cliff face of almost 100 ft to the north and west. To the south and south-east the land falls gently into the Teme valley, and it was on these slopes that the streets of the medieval planned settlement were laid out. The castle, which dominated the town, was started soon after the

*45   Kilpeck (Hereford and
     Worcester) with its
     castle in the centre and
     the fortified abandoned
     settlement clearly
     showing below it*

Conquest and it seems likely that the first town streets were laid out within a decade or so after this. A hundred years later, in 1199, there was a large church on the site of the present parish church of St Lawrence.

By 1200 the process of town creation and development was well advanced. Undoubtedly, the overall level of European trading prosperity would have overflowed into England even without the Normans, but the scale of urbanisation may not have been so great. The Norman town was an important instrument of political, strategic administrative and economic control. The Normans found them flexible enough both to exert control over its hinterland and to exploit it commercially. Towns that the Normans originally created to dominate a region politically and strategically were later adapted to become the major commercial and trading centres (**47a** and **b**).

French colonies

A feature of many early town foundations was that French boroughs or colonies of French traders were often established alongside English settlements. Sometimes these were located in already existing urban settlements, such as Stamford, Nottingham and Hereford. At Hereford, French settlers were introduced by William Fitz Osbern, who granted them the customs of Breteuil sur Iton (Eure), while the English community maintained their ancient burghal customs. Later, the Breteuil customs were widely adopted by boroughs in western England and Wales. In the first instance, at Hereford,

1   *Aerial view of the Iron Age and Viking settlement at Jarlshof in the Shetlands*

2   *Aerial view of the Seine valley in Normandy, Vikings wintered on the island of Jenfosse in 853 and 856*

H·S·E·GVILLELMVS·LONGA·DICTVS·SPATHA
...IAM·QVI·SVIS·ROLLONIS·FILIVS·STATVIT·IN·FINIBVS
...VM·INSIDIIS·ANNO·CM·XLII·OCCISVS

3   *William Longsword's tomb dating from the thirteenth century, in Rouen Cathedral*

4   *Abbey Saint George at*
     Boscherville on the River
     Seine to the west of Rouen

5   *Duke Robert I, William the Conqueror's father, from a twelfth-century manuscript*

6   *View of William the Conqueror's Abbey church of St Stephen's, Caen*

7 *The twelfth-century and later castle at Falaise, on the site of an earlier castle where William the Conqueror was born*

8 *Site of the battle of Val-ès Dunes where William defeated his rebellious barons*

9   The castle of Arques-la-Battaille, the scene of critical battles in the eleventh and twelfth centuries

*10   The western façade of
Jumièges Abbey*

11 Reconstruction of Norman Westminster Abbey

12 St Valery-Sur-Somme, the place from whence the invasion force sailed for England

13   Soldiers foraging in the vicinity of Hastings before the Battle of Hastings in a scene from the
Bayeux Tapestry, Norman

14   The death of King Harold depicted on the Bayeux Tapestry

15 *Chepstow Castle, near the estuary of the River Wye. William Fitz Osbern's stronghold in southern Wales*

16 *Archbishop Lanfranc from a twelfth-century document*

17   *The Norman exchequer building in Caen castle*

18   *Norwich Castle, one of the great Norman palace castles, largely refaced during the nineteenth century*

19 *Gisors Castle, a motte with a shell keep on top of it. It lies in the Norman Vexin, and was the scene of prolonged dispute between the Normans and the French king during the second half of the twelfth century*

20 *Extract from Domesday Book for Herefordshire*

21 *Aerial view of Cefnllys, an abandoned hill fort town in Wales*

22 *Eleventh-century manuscript depicting a harpist*

23 *Moslem siege of Messina, Sicily in the ninth century*

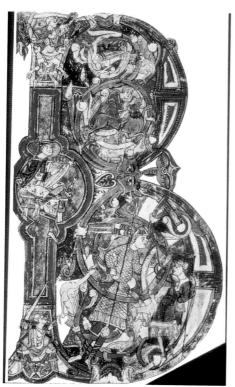

26 The west front of Troia cathedral, Apulia

24 (far left) Twelfth-century illustrated manuscript from Winchester

25 (left) Hauteville-la-Guichard, the village in the Cotentin peninsula, home of the Hauteville family who dominated Sicily and southern Italy during the eleventh and twelfth centuries

27 *Medieval manuscript showing Arabic cultivation of sugar cane*

28 *The east end of San Annuaziata, Messina*

29 King Roger's silk coronation mantle

30 William the Good
presenting the cathedral at
Monreale to the Virgin
Mary

31   *The west front of the cathedral with its two great twin towers*

32   *Cefalu, showing the regulated layout of the town*

46   *The regular grid
plan of Bury St
Edmunds, Suffolk,
with the ruins of the
Abbey towards the
centre bottom of the
picture. The town
was in the process
of being laid out
when the Domesday
Book was compiled*

there seems to have been a geographical separation of the two communities and their markets, but gradually English and French customs were welded together. There were 'French boroughs' in a number of other towns, including Pontefract, Ludlow and Richmond (Yorks).

At Nottingham, William the Conqueror established a castle and borough alongside an existing Anglo-Scandinavian town. The French borough, as it continued to be called, was an appendage to the English borough, but with its own defences, streets and church. Within the new circuit of defences, encompassing some 120 acres, the northern and western walls of the Saxon *burh* were abandoned and by 1086 the ditch had been built over, but the distinction survived throughout the Middle Ages, each borough having its own sheriff and bailiff. The inheritance practices prevailing in both parts remained quite distinctive, that in the English *burh* still being 'borough English' rather than the usual primogeniture. The situation in Nottingham underlines William's psychology and strategy; the area was one of considerable royal interest, not least because of its close proximity to Sherwood Forest. Firstly, William was intent upon establishing a dominant Norman presence with a castle and a borough and secondly, although the Anglian city may have been detached and partially completed, it was not entirely destroyed, and thus William utilised the amenities already available. Thirdly, he was able to operate links that had existed prior to the Conquest, when Nottingham was the centre of a loose federation of five boroughs in an area with strong Scandinavian mercantile influence.

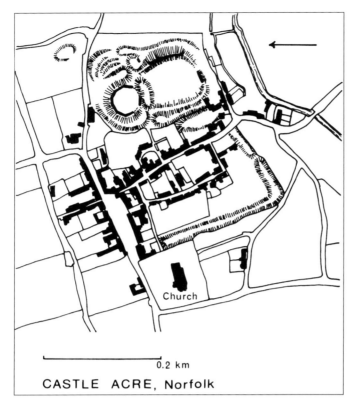

47(a) *Castle Acre, Norfolk, plan of the castle borough*

0.2 km

CASTLE ACRE, Norfolk

The Anglo-Norman church

Between 1070 and 1087, under the control of William, the English church experienced great changes which partly echoed events that had previously taken place in the province of Rouen. Tangible links between the English and French church were immediately strengthened; the Conqueror paid his debt to Valéry, the Picard saint, for the favourable breeze that blew him to England before the battle of Hastings, by granting the manor of Tackley in Essex to Valéry priory. The following year, Hayling Island was granted to the monks of Jumièges to celebrate the consecration of their new abbey church. William founded Battle Abbey on the site where the English had fought, with the high altar marking the spot where King Harold had fallen. Traditionally, the abbey was said to have been founded as a result of a vow made by Duke William before the battle in which he promised to establish a monastery free from Episcopal control if God granted him victory. It seems more probable that William's vow was made c.1070, the year he was formally re-crowned by papal legates, and papal authorities imposed heavy penances on the Normans for the bloodshed of the invasion and subsequent pacification of England. Initially he housed the abbey with monks from Marmoutier on the Loire. Because of the difficulties of building on such an irregular site the monastery was not finally consecrated until 1094 (**48**). On his death, the Conqueror had bequeathed to the community at Battle his royal cloak, a collection of relics and a portable altar used during his military campaigns. More

47(b)   Aerial view of a castle borough at Castle Acre, Norfolk

important than these were the estates he granted to the abbey, which made it one of the wealthiest in the country, together with widespread immunity from secular authority. Altogether, nearly 30 Norman monasteries received gifts of manors, estates, churches and tithes in England during the decade subsequent to the Conquest.

Although the Normans were awed by the English church and its traditions, they were often sceptical about its customs and culture and they coveted its wealth. They disliked its archaic Roman liturgy, its buildings, constructed in what they regarded as an outmoded style, and its incomprehensible learning. Initially, Normans had little respect for the English saints, and Archbishop Lanfranc wrote: 'These Englishmen among whom we are living have set up for themselves certain saints whom they revere. But sometimes when I turn over in my mind their own accounts of whom they were, I cannot help having doubts about the quality of their sanctity'. With less circumspection, Lanfranc's kinsman, Abbot Paul, broke the tombs of the former abbots of St Albans whom he referred to as 'uncultured idiots'. The new abbot of Abingdon tried to obliterate the memory of St Æthelwold, whom he called 'an English rustic', while at Evesham Abbot Walter (1077–1104) put the saints' relics to the test by fire — only those that survived were deemed to be genuine. This hostility to the English saints did not survive the first generation of Norman clerics; the writings of contemporary chroniclers did much to re-establish the reputation of the most famous saints and the church began to appreciate the financial importance of their Saxon relics in attracting pilgrims.

William needed bishops whom he could trust absolutely and who could serve as vice-regents in his newly-won kingdom. He delayed only a few years before instigating a radical re-staffing of the English church and, prompted by clerical involvement in the northern uprisings, William set about the systematic replacement of the upper sections of the Anglo-Saxon church hierarchy. In 1069 the Saxon Stigand, so vilified by the Normans,

48   *Aerial view of Battle Abbey. Little remains of the Norman foundation, and after the dissolution some of the abbey buildings were incorporated into a residential house, now a school. However, the central area of the photograph was where Harold's English army stood while being attacked by the Normans (bottom left). At the top of the picture, evidence of the Norman town of Battle which grew up at the abbey gates*

was at last removed as Archbishop of Canterbury and replaced by William's friend and confidant, Lanfranc. Thereafter Normans and continental clerics were appointed steadily as offices fell vacant. These were men chosen for their administrative capabilities rather than their spiritual strength. So complete was the eventual foreign 'take-over' of English institutions that William of Malmesbury, writing in about 1125, claimed that 'England has become a residence for foreigners and the property of aliens. At the present time there is no English earl, nor bishop nor abbot; strangers all, they prey upon the riches and vitals of England.' The semi-religious nature of the Conquest 'involved the Saxon church in ecclesiastical censure of the unfortunate Harold and contributed to render the Norman Conquest as complete intellectually as it was politically.' William and his immediate successors pursued a vigorous policy not only of appointing non-English archbishops, bishops and abbots, but also of radically restructuring the organisation of the church. The spiritual jurisdiction, which bishops and arch-deacons had only been able to exercise through the temporal courts, was transferred to new ecclesiastical courts, which were answerable to the synod. The synod, which sat regularly under Lanfranc, and the church in England received the same legislative and judicial independence that it enjoyed in France. During his tenure of the see at Canterbury Lanfranc revealed talents for diplomacy, administration and politics which were at least equal to his talent for teaching. For all his piety and enthusiasm for monasticism and his instinctive obedience to Rome, his loyalty to William, in the last resort, was stronger than his commitment to the papacy. William's relations with Pope Gregory VII, who succeeded Alexander II in 1073, were blighted over the issues of clerical marriage, the claim of papal sovereignty over William and the withdrawal of the right to invest bishops. Lanfranc's advocacy on behalf of William effectively meant that William was able to ignore these papal decrees, and when war broke out between the Papacy and the Holy Roman Empire England remained neutral.

Lanfranc, apart from being a resourceful politician, was also a sincere churchman and confirmed ecclesiastical reformer. He brought with him to England a group of pupils and associates from the monasteries at Bec and Caen, most of whom were destined for promotion to high places. They included his nephew Paul, who became the abbot of St Albans, Gundulf, subsequently Bishop of Rochester and surveyor of the king's works at the Tower of London, and Gilbert Crispin, who became abbot of Westminster. Within ten years of the Conquest, all the English bishoprics, with the exception of Worcester, were in the hands of continental clerics.

William and Archbishop Lanfranc shared the concept of a sharp hierarchical structure and insisted that Canterbury had primacy, not only over England, but also over the whole British Isles. A council at Windsor, held in 1072, decreed that each rural see should be moved to a major town in its diocese. This policy had many implications, particularly as the ancient centres were often closely associated with saints' relics. The see at Dorchester-on-Thames was transferred to Lincoln, Sherborne to Old Sarum, Selsey to Chichester, Elmham to Norwich by way of Thetford, Wells to Bath and Lichfield to Chester. Although there were subsequent readjustments — Henry I created a new diocese in each province, Ely in Canterbury and Carlisle in York — those moves established the basic diocesan framework of England for many centuries. Additionally, bishops were ordered to appoint proper ecclesiastical officials and the dioceses were divided into archdeaconries —

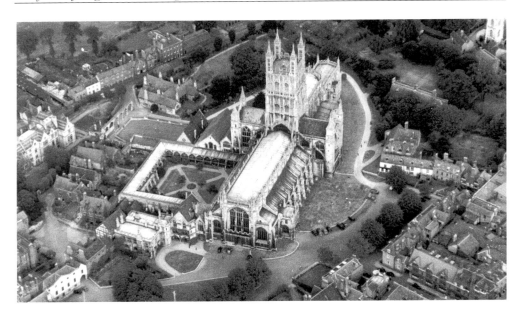

49   *Aerial view of Gloucester Abbey, essentially a medieval Gothic building incorporating a Norman core and a very Norman crypt. It was here that Robert Curthose, William the Conqueror's eldest son, was buried*

which were eventually subdivided into rural deaneries, thereby establishing the pattern of ecclesiastical territories up to the Reformation and beyond. Whereas the Roman administrative centres survived in Normandy up until the French Revolution, in England it was the Normans who created the basic ecclesiastical administrative network.

Despite the reorganisation of the secular church, the essentially monastic character of the tenth-century reformation under St Dunstan survived the Conquest and gave rise to the peculiarly British custom of establishing a bishop's see in a monastic church. In eight of the Norman dioceses the cathedral was a monastic church, the bishop being considered as the abbot and the prior the head of the working monastery. One immediate result of this reorganisation was that the secular church was able to build on the same scale as the great Benedictine monasteries and the cathedrals began to compete with large monastic churches in their architectural achievements (**49**).

The cultural affinities between the Anglo-Norman ruling classes and the French homelands from whence the majority of the monastic institutions originated meant that there was an easy transition from mainland Europe to England. The radical distribution of land after 1066 provided ample resources for the spread of monasticism. The Conquest resulted in the concentration both of land and of wealth within the hands of a small group of Normans. Overnight it had turned many of them from being local manorial lords into great magnates and they found they had a considerable surplus to their accustomed wealth and land. Traditionally and diplomatically pious by nature, they spent a percentage of this surplus on the endowment of churches and cathedrals, and some of the surplus land, most frequently that which was of marginal agricultural value at the time of endowment, was painlessly given to the newly founded monasteries in order to ensure a place in heaven.

The first impetus of church building included new cathedrals at Worcester, Rochester and St Albans, but in the first instance there were relatively few monasteries; Battle, Lewes and Shrewsbury were notable exceptions. Within 50 years of the Conquest, work had also started on hundreds of small priories and parish churches, often built close by lordly manors or castles. There was a dramatic change in the character of church dedications after 1066. Saxon dedications virtually ceased and continental saints' names became increasingly common, with dedications to saints such as Catherine, Stephen and Michael replacing those to Anglo-Saxon and Celtic saints. Additionally, many existing Saxon churches were rededicated to saints more familiar to the Normans in the century or so after the conquest.

Royal forests

One of the charges levelled against the Norman kings, both by contemporary chroniclers and later historians, was that they imposed a draconian system of forest law over much of England. The Anglo-Saxon Chronicle for 1087 claims that: 'The King, William, set up great protection for deer and legislated to that intent that who so ever should slay hart or hind should be blinded … He loved the high deer as if he were their father.' At one stage in the twelfth century, royal forest subject to Norman forest law covered up to a third of England. This legal structure was quite distinct from the Anglo-Norman common law.

Pre-Norman kings hunted and created game reserves for the purpose, but these areas were not forests in the legal sense. However, a twelfth-century forgery attributing the forest laws to King Cnut was used to imply their Saxon pedigree and, indeed, Cnut had laid a heavy fine on anyone who hunted in a district he had set apart for his own pleasure. Moreover, Edward the Confessor maintained a system of forest wardens. Therefore, although the Saxons actually had no word for forest, the concept of the king's wood was not a new one. Kingswood, in the Weald of Kent, was so called from the mid-Saxon period, and specific areas such as Woodstock Chase in Oxfordshire had been reserved for Saxon kings.

Forest law was gradually tightened up during the twelfth century and only began to weaken after 1216, when the Crown could no longer withstand the antagonism that the forest law and its officials caused among its subjects. It is doubtful, however, whether the forest laws were ever quite as harsh as they appear in contemporary description. Certainly by the thirteenth century a considerable degree of latitude had crept into their implementation. Many of the fines for encroachment were no more than an annual rental, and fines imposed for tree felling in reality represented a form of trading.

The full royal forest system was only in its infancy at the Conqueror's death (1087), by which time only about a quarter of the eventual royal forests had been created. The Domesday record of 25 forests, although incomplete, clearly indicates that the process had far to go. Many forests, such as Sherwood (1154) and Epping (1130), are not heard of until the twelfth century, and there appears to have been a third phase of afforestation under Richard I, which probably includes the Neroche Forest (Somerset) which was not mentioned until 1221.

The New Forest in Hampshire was so called because it represented an unprecedented extension of forest jurisdiction. It is also popular legend that an extensive area of Hampshire was depopulated for the benefit of the newly introduced deer. This theory has been disputed by many authorities who argue that the degree of disturbance was relatively minor. We can trace the extension of Windsor forest from the time of the Conquest, at which stage it appears to have been limited to the Windsor area. By 1086 William had considerably extended the bounds, as can be seen from several Domesday entries. By the middle of the twelfth century it covered most of Berkshire, Buckinghamshire, Oxfordshire, Middlesex and Surrey, and by the thirteenth century it even extended into Hampshire. However, as a result of a forest perambulation held in 1225 to decide which parts should be disafforested, only the original area in the immediate vicinity of Windsor remained as forest.

The largest physical forests were the New Forest, with about 80,000 acres of heath and woodland, and Sherwood, with about 50,000 acres of woodland. Several, such as Weybridge (Huntingdonshire) or Hatfield (Essex), had as little as 1000 acres of woodland pasture, while others such as Chute (Wiltshire) appear to have been merely fragmented patches of woodland with no identifiable nucleus. At a rough estimate, at its fullest extent the legal forest jurisdiction, royal and private, covered a third of the country, compared to the physical woodland forest which probably covered little more than 15% of the whole of England in the twelfth century.

In a major review of early medieval forest-land, Oliver Rackham has recorded at least 142 forests in England, some of which, such as the Forest of Arden (Warwickshire), are poorly documented. The Crown controlled 86 of these. The forest was the supreme status symbol for the noblest of families, such as the earls of Richmond, and amongst churchmen only the bishops of Durham and Winchester achieved proprietorial rights. In Cheshire the forests of Wirral, Delamere, Mondrem and Macclesfield were all in the hands of earls. We should perhaps note that the term 'chase' is inconsistently used to distinguish the forest of a subject from that of the crown.

It has been argued that the Norman monarchs regarded deer hunting not merely as a royal hobby but as an essential business, a form of subsistence farming to support the court, and consequently they needed to introduce special laws to protect the deer. The early medieval kings and their courts relied heavily on game as an important food source and were prepared to devote much of their territory to its protection. The itineraries of the court demonstrate that their main concern was to remain close to the principal supplies of royal venison. Despite the Norman kings' reputed love of the chase, references to the king hunting in person are surprisingly few, and normally the task of killing the deer was undertaken by professional huntsmen. From the middle of the twelfth century, the Pipe Rolls refer to large quantities of venison killed and the preservation of meat by salting and its transportation.

The Normans introduced fallow deer from the Levant or Near East as a means of producing meat from poor agricultural land. The rabbit and pheasant, which have comparable histories, are other relics of Norman enterprise in providing alternatives to agriculture and cattle breeding in otherwise agriculturally unprofitable areas. Fallow deer are not mentioned as one of William the Conqueror's favourite animals in his obituary in

50 Sketch plan of Rosamund's Bower in Woodstock Park by John Aubrey (seventeenth century). This was an exotic twelfth-century garden with springs and pools, whose design was possibly inspired by contemporary gardens in Sicily

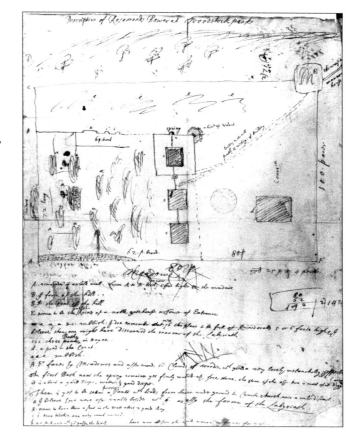

the Anglo-Saxon Chronicle of 1087, and it has been surmised that they were first introduced in the early twelfth century as part of the second phase of park and forest creation. One possible source would have been via the Sicilian connection. The conquest of Sicily after 1060 brought the Normans into contact with the classical and Islamic traditions of emparking and the keeping of beasts. Whatever their country of origin, the fallow deer were an immediate success in England (**50**).

The royal forests were most extensive in the late twelfth century, and by the mid-thirteenth century when records of individual forests become plentiful they were already in decline. Although the process of disafforestation was a protracted one, extending over many centuries up to the nineteenth century, and many of the legal and administrative trappings survived throughout the Middle Ages, the true royal forests were a relatively short-lived feature in the landscape. Only the Norman kings at the very height of their authority could have imposed and maintained such a system, and thus the forest should be seen very much as a phenomenon of Norman England.

6 Aspects of Anglo-Norman society

In some ways the world the Normans inhabited was more cosmopolitan than our own. State and principality boundaries were constantly moving and rarely policed. This meant that people's movements between territories were rarely restricted by ethnic or political considerations. The cosmopolitan nature of European society was particularly evident at the courtly level where intermarriage between the different ruling groups was not only common, but was expected. Accordingly, many aspects of eleventh and twelfth-century life, particularly in the areas of music and literature, were not restricted to one country or another, but were found throughout Europe, albeit with regional variations.

In the area of social manners, Normans were regarded as a 'rude and somewhat barbarous people'. It is probably true, in the words of Stenton, that the Normans, 'had produced little in art or learning in literature that could be set beside the work of an Englishman.' But Anglo-Norman society was subject to a cultural blend incorporating indigenous English as well as continental elements, out of which came considerable artistic and literary achievements. The Italian clerics, Lanfranc and Anselm (**51**), were particularly important examples of the cosmopolitan influence in the church. With regard to luxuries and refinements in material culture, most Norman barons lived much as their Anglo-Saxon predecessors had done only perhaps more lavishly, but there is little evidence of conspicuous consumption by the first generation or so of Norman lords.

Anglo-Saxons and Normans

Despite the very clear evidence of Norman control there were relatively few Normans in England after the Conquest, probably no more than 50,000 compared to a native population of perhaps 2 million. Accordingly it was inevitable that Norman domination was largely confined to the upper echelons of society. Although groups of French settlers did move into England and founded colonies in a number of towns, the level of folk penetration was far less even than that perpetrated by the tenth-century Norsemen in Normandy, and cannot be compared in scale to the Germanic migration in the post Roman period. Indeed, recent analysis of place names in Normandy suggests that there may even have been a modest movement of English settlers into Normandy after the Conquest. Similarly, Englishmen participated in the movement south and east on pilgrimages or as mercenary soldiers. Among the far-flung places the English found themselves in the wake of the Conquest was Constantinople where there was a small expatriate community.

The men who came to England with William were mainly drawn from the area round Rouen, but others included some Bretons (who settled primarily in the south-west and in the Honour of Richmond), some from the Cotentin peninsular, and sub-tenants of powerful men such as Odo of Bayeux. The distinction between the French and English intensified social cleavage as the French were protected in Norman law far more than the

51   *Romanesque corbel table, Romsey Abbey, one of the wealthiest nunneries in England. It was from here that Henry I's wife, Edith came.*

English right down the social scale. The Norman distinction between knight and villein was much greater than the Saxon difference between thegn and count, and the development of the aristocratic household reflected the imposition of feudalism on the country. The king granted fiefs to barons who in return owed a number of knights. The fief, held together by a manorial court, was shared out amongst military sub-tenants and a hierarchy formed even amongst them. The lower grades of society were uniformly called *villani* — this was not a derogatory term during the early stages and did not become so until the mid-twelfth century.

Slaves were possibly less profitable than 'free' peasants bound to give hard labour service to their lord, and, perhaps surprisingly, slavery was abolished in Norman England. Indeed, the Domesday survey records that as much as 12% of the population in 1086 were categorised as slaves. There had been several slave markets in England; perhaps the best known one was in Bristol, which carried out a thriving trade with Ireland. By the end of the twelfth century slaves had virtually disappeared from the records. As late as the 1120s the church was able to decree a reduction in status as a suitable punishment for clerical concubines. It was, perhaps, because the Norman lord regarded his tenants as his own men and he had rights over all the people on his lands that the formal category of slavery became less important. The tendency was for all the peasantry to be characterised as *villani*, which reflected the diminished status of most agricultural workers. Additionally, the principal characteristics of a freeman, the right to bear arms and the right to testify on oath before the courts, also diminished in status under Norman feudalism.

Anglo-Norman women

In the post Conquest period women enjoyed a lower status in both the law and the church than their Anglo-Saxon predecessors. The newly imposed code of Anglo-Norman feudal law and the development and codification of canon law both reduced women's legal rights. The legal status of a woman of any social class depended on whether she was single or married. Single or widowed, she could exercise the same private legal rights as a man; married, her rights were extinguished, and her person as well as her goods, lands and chattels fell under her husband's control. She regained her own estate and dowry only upon her husband's death, with the addition of a lifetime share of a portion of his estate.

The adoption of primogeniture (inheritance by the eldest male child) as the main pattern for legacies tended to disqualify noble women from any share in the family wealth, except for their dowry. However, townswomen and peasants were less tied by such rigid inheritance patterns. In all classes, though most prominently in the nobility, the wealthy widow often found herself with remarkable freedom of action. Despite their private rights, women had no right to hold office or to exercise public authority. Canon law, which dealt with both marriages and wills, reflected the clerical conviction concerning the inferiority of women and their need to be under male authority. Nevertheless, it insisted on their right to accept freely their marriage partners, and it also denied the right to force children into marriage under the age of consent (12 for girls, 14 for boys). Canon law also consistently encouraged the making of wills, even by married women who technically had no power to do so without their husband's consent.

Conditions on the ground frequently contradicted the legal theory. Feudal lords were often absent, and their wives found themselves in charge of large households with a full complement of officials, knights and men-at-arms, fighting legal battles over rights to lands, and maintaining adequate military strength to protect their castles or manorial houses. The rapid development of towns and their fast-growing populations in the twelfth century also opened new doors for townswomen who were allowed to join most craft guilds. Women's right to conduct business on their own behalf, even when married, was embodied in commercial law.

English nunneries were not as rich or as populous as the religious houses for men, but they provided a respectable alternative to marriage for the upper classes. Some houses, such as the priories at Amesbury, Shaftesbury and Romsey, grew rich with royal patronage and attracted aristocratic women. Some of the English aristocracy decided that life in a nunnery was preferable to a forced marriage to a Norman lord and there was a modest rise in numbers of nuns as a result of the Conquest (**51**).

Anglo-Norman language and names

There is little evidence of totally new settlements linked to Norman colonisation in post Conquest England, apart from new villages in the north in those areas devastated during the harrying of the north and William Rufus' campaigns in the north-west. Accordingly there were few completely new Norman place names, although Norman French place name elements are common. The place name evidence demonstrates a similar pattern of hybridisation to that which had occurred in Normandy in the tenth century. Norman family names were attached to already existing Anglo-Saxon place names such as Cleobury Mortimer (Salop), Langton Maltravers (Dorset) or Ascot D'Oilly (Oxon). Norman owners frequently gave French names to castles and manors, while Norman monks provided French names for monasteries and granges. These names were frequently descriptive in character; *Beau (Belle)* is a particularly common element in, for instance, Beaumont (beautiful hill) and Bellevoir (beautiful view); Riveaulx (Yorks) is a French translation of Ryedale.

English survived as a vernacular language, much enriched by Latin and French after the Conquest. The language of literature changed too, from early English to Latin. In Edward the Confessor's time, the Anglo-Saxon Chronicle had been kept up at some half-dozen monasteries and, in a few, it survived the coming of the Normans, although Latin rapidly gained ground over the vernacular. About the year 1100 a version of the Chronicle was copied bilingually at St Augustine's, Canterbury. Another, at Christchurch, Canterbury, retained the native language until 1110 when it started to be written in Latin with occasional English entries. Another version, compiled at St Augustine's and then at Peterborough, continued in English right up until the accession of Henry II in 1154.

Latin was the language of the church, of scholars, of government and of the law by the twelfth century, but it was a Latin that had been infiltrated by French and English words. Nevertheless, Latin was a language enjoyed only by the few men of letters, the clergy and by civil servants; the Norman court spoke French and the great bulk of the population English. Occasionally documents are bilingual; a writ of Henry II confirming the privileges of London to Bishop Anselm, for example. Sometimes, estate boundaries were described in Anglo-Saxon even as late as the reign of Henry II. English was also still used in county courts in the first decades of the twelfth century.

English was undoubtedly spoken, even in aristocratic Norman households. Many Normans took English wives, and it is reasonable to assume that a large section of society, even of the nobility, was bilingual. Many of the higher clergy spoke and preached in English, and it is said that 'the pulpit was the cradle of English prose'. Indeed, it was devotional literature in the vernacular that preserved the tradition of English prose writing during the Anglo-Norman period. At Worcester, owing to the influence of the English Bishop Wulfstan who held the see until 1095 and whose own life was written by a Worcester monk in Anglo-Saxon, the persistence of the native language in religious works was particularly strong. Collections of sermons, Anglo-Saxon versions of sections of the Bible, service books and lives of saints continued to be copied there in the twelfth century. However, Old French gained rapidly over English as the language of Romance poetry, commerce and architecture.

Anglo-Saxon personal names fell out of fashion and were replaced by Norman alternatives, which were primarily of French or continental German origin, and a little later with Biblical names, which had been rare in Saxon England. In Winchester, for example, Norman personal names were soon to be in the majority after the Conquest, as they were widely adopted by the Anglo-Norman population.

Anglo-Norman literature

The growth and influence of Anglo-Norman literature should be seen against the broad cultural relationship between Normandy and England, beginning in the decades before the Conquest. The influence was two-way: Norman art and sculpture show the influence of English design and English skills in such differing areas as coinage and embroidery and these were preserved by the Conqueror. The vernacular literature of Anglo-Saxon England was established and highly developed with an output unequalled by any other European vernacular. In contrast Norman literature was almost non-existent, although after the Conquest Norman writers turned to Anglo-Saxon literature, law and cultural traditions for inspiration and information. Anglo-Saxon writing provided the Normans with a plentiful source for serious, high-quality literature, written in the vernacular for the education and entertainment of the aristocracy.

Post Conquest England encompassed a tri-lingual culture. Latin, being the international language of the Church and scholarship, was introduced as the language of government by the Norman kings in place of English. French became the language of the rulers and of polite society, but gradually altered from the French spoken on the continent. English was effectively relegated to third place as a literary language. In the post Conquest period, authors writing in Anglo-Norman were using source material in English, Latin and perhaps Welsh, while later writers in English drew on French or Latin material. The choice of language was dictated by the taste of the expected audience or patron, or by the nature of the topic. More significantly language was not yet perceived as part of national identity. The material moves easily from one vernacular to another within the same manuscript or even within the same poem. This flexibility is demonstrated by the large intake of romance vocabulary into English throughout the Anglo-Norman period and means that its literary influence is pervasive rather than distinctive. Anglo-Norman literature develops more through its response to Latin than to English, often representing the popularisation of more scholarly Latin writing.

The literature of the first century after the Conquest is small in quantity but significantly ahead of developments on the continent (**colour plate 24**). From its beginning, Anglo-Norman narrative literature presents the ecclesiastical and secular rulers of Anglo-Norman England with material about the land they now ruled. This perspective is first apparent in the work of the early twelfth-century historians in England and Normandy, for instance, William of Malmesbury, Henry of Huntingdon and Orderic Vitalis. In 1155 the Norman poet Wace completed his *Roman de Brut*, a highly influential account of British history which was later translated into English. He then moved on to Norman history with the less well-known and less successful *Roman de Rue, c.*1160–70.

Anglo-Norman literature flourished in the reign of Henry II when the Angevin court claimed to be the dominant literary centre of Europe. The Angevin succession, together with the inheritance of Aquitaine, placed England within an empire which extended from the Welsh Marches to the Pyrenees and gave access to all the cultural diversity associated with those lands. The Anglo-Norman *Tristan* of Thomas was the most striking of the new literary achievements. Its sympathetic account of doomed and passionate adultery and the absence of judgmental elements commonly found in other medieval writings meant that contemporary literary reaction was largely negative, although historical criticism has been much kinder. Some of the major narrative works of the following decades have been interpreted as being responses to the morality of *Tristan*. Nevertheless, the story of Tristan and Isolde spread to become one of the classical statements of passionate love in European literature.

Much early literature was written for the immediate circle of the peripatetic, cosmopolitan royal court, but at the same time there was a development of romance written for baronial patrons. This was written for a more provincial audience with elaborate treatment of the so-called 'matter of England romances', partly based on genuine Anglo-Saxon or Scandinavian legend. Largely fictional work such as *Haveloc the Dane* and *Romance of Horne* represent the finest products of this genre. *Boeve de Hauntone* and *Guy de Warewic* are evidently connected with the family interest of the owners of Arundel Castle, and the earls of Warwick respectively. Both were later translated into English for wider audience. Such romances demonstrated in their plots the broader interests of an incoming feudal dynasty, the hero acquiring lands by marriage with an heiress, holding his own in conflict with the centralising power of the monarchy and borrowing the names and geography of England to establish authenticity.

Alongside secular narratives, saints' histories also developed. These stories were written for monastic and lay audiences, generally with courtly taste and an interest in tales of those pre-conquest saints who had shrines in the new cathedrals. The patronage of successive queens supported such twelfth-century works as Benedeit's *Voyage of St Brendan*, a colourful account of the Celtic saint's miraculous journeys, and Dennis Pyramis's *Life of St Edmund*. Drama also evolved in the twelfth century with the *Jeu d'Adam* and the *Seinte Resurrection*, two liturgical plays showing a high level of literary ability and conscious stagecraft.

Historical writing in the vernacular continued in the late twelfth and thirteenth centuries with the *Brut* tradition of British history, lively accounts of contemporary events such as Jordan Fantosme's *Chronique* and *The Scottish Wars of Henry II*, a heroic play on the conquest of Ireland, and a popular biography of Richard I. The Anglo-Norman literary tradition did not, of course, stop with the Plantagenets, and it continued even into the fifteenth century. To the time of Chaucer and beyond the royal court continued to keep up with the dominant fashions of France, but outside that circle, in the baronial halls, manor houses and monasteries in England, the literary development of chronicled romance and saints' lives provided a continuing tradition of vernacular provincial writing.

Music in Anglo-Norman society

During the years of the Norman ascendancy, musical life was largely dominated by liturgical influence. The tradition at the abbey of Cluny was the primary source for Norman liturgical practices relative to the celebration of the mass and of sacred offices. This Cluniac practice was exported by the Normans to the countries they conquered. Liturgical drama and secular music, in the form of songs, either unaccompanied or accompanied by bowed or plucked instruments, drums or pipes, was also an important part of Norman life, especially among the aristocracy. The vernacular texts set in these

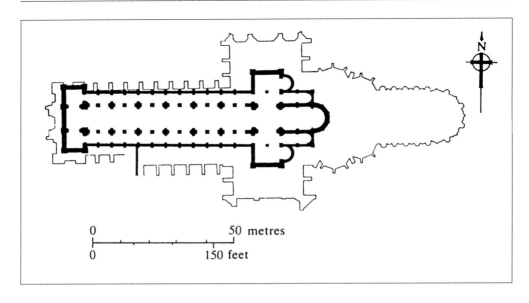

52   *Plan showing the comparative size of Edward the Confessor's Abbey church at Westminster compared to the church today*

songs trace the intermingling of conquerors and conquered so typical of the Norman pattern of invasion followed by assimilation. It would appear that in their music, as in so many other things, the Normans both influenced and were influenced by what they encountered in the countries they invaded. This phenomenon of mutual influence is a major contributing factor in the relative homogeneity of style that characterises this period in western music history.

The music of the church, in the form of settings of the mass and office, followed practices established at Cluny, the recognised source of 'correct' liturgical practice. As the Normans conquered other lands they replaced the local officials, both ecclesiastical and secular, with their own. For example, the 'most powerful impact of the Conquest on liturgical music (in England) came from the wholesale replacement of senior monastic officials by Norman monks, with a resulting Norman influence in liturgy, ceremonial and chant in which the practices of Cluny and Bec were particularly important'. But even as they exported their own practices, the Normans also assimilated local practice. Again, the Conquest of England provides an example: 'Eleventh-century English and Norman monks also continued the tenth-century Benedictine literary and musical tradition of writing hymns, sequences and full rhymed offices for Anglo-Saxon saints' and 'many continental tropes [additional texts set to music interpolated into existing Mass texts as commentaries] have been re-worked texturally and musically in a campaign of re-composition to suit local needs and tastes'.

53(a)   The remarkable blind arcading on the western front at Castle Acre Priory

Liturgical music

Mass and office settings, always of Latin texts, were largely monophonic, with one voice line, but examples of simple note against note polyphony of two or more voices also survive. Later on, in the period of Norman ascendancy, liturgical music was influenced by practices and the musical repertory of the cathedral at Notre Dame in Paris. These practices were centred on the two-voice polyphony for all major feasts of the church year set out in the famous source, *Magnus liber*, composed by Leonin in the 1170s and early 1180s. The Normans and those they ruled surely must have heard these mass and office settings as well as the liturgical dramas associated with the celebration of the Nativity and the Resurrection. Based on the Biblical story of the 'empty tomb' and the question *quem queritas?* that asks where the resurrected one had been taken, this drama typically consists of alternating sung lines and voices and was performed in monasteries throughout northern France before the closing hymn in the service of Matins. Other liturgical dramas, including the Magi plays and Easter Pilgrims' plays, abounded during this time. The texts and music were characterised by a regular rhyme scheme and systematic melodies that combined poetry with distinct melodies. These liturgical dramas provide a 'bridge' from the purely liturgical, Latin-texted music to the non-liturgical and, sometimes, vernacular-texted medieval songs that were doubtless also heard and performed by the Normans.

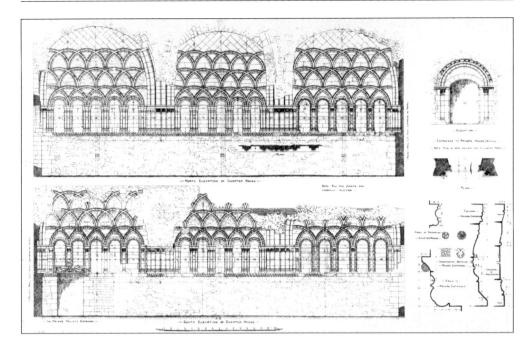

53(b)   The blind arcading in the Chapter House at Wenlock Priory from the 'Builder' August, 1888

Non-liturgical music

Non-liturgical music extant at the time of Norman ascendancy comprises devotional and quasi-sacred songs, secular songs and instrumental pieces. Song texts were in the vernacular, and a consideration of such texts reveals that there was considerable influence both from the Normans to those they conquered and vice versa. For example, although there was what Lefferts calls 'a wider musical culture embracing Anglo-Norman England and northern France' there was, as time went on, a 'drift of Anglo-Norman away from mainland French dialects, and [this was] a process for which one can find parallels in politics, the fine arts, architecture, and music'. In England 'the first hundred years of Norman rule saw the introduction at the highest level of society of a new vernacular with its own tradition of secular entertainment music. These included Anglo-Norman and Middle English verse chronicles, epics, [and] romances'. Devotional monophonic Latin songs were also written, and the monastic rhymed Offi for St Thomas of Canterbury, written in the late 1170s, continued that Anglo-Saxon and early Norman tradition of writing in this form and to Latin text. While Latin remained the language of choice for most non-liturgical devotional songs, French was the language of social intercourse and literature among the aristocracy in England after the Conquest. Therefore, the ubiquitous romance song both in Normandy and in Britain at this time invariably had a French or Anglo-Norman text. Songs were both unaccompanied and accompanied by plucked and/or bowed instruments (e.g., by *harpa* or early lute and/or viols, pipes and drums) (**colour plate 22**).

*54   Reconstruction of the Norman Minster church at Southwell. The twin western and the
central towers, together with the eastern apsidal chapels, are typical of late eleventh-century
Norman buildings*

In the period of ascendancy, the Normans were accustomed to a range of music both liturgical and secular; nearly everyone would have been exposed to sung masses, offices and liturgical drama set to Latin texts. Members of the upper classes and aristocracy would have also enjoyed secular and devotional songs, set to Latin and/or vernacular texts, and instrumental music as entertainment. Music of the times was relatively simple in that there was often only one voice part, monophany, and this was usually unaccompanied. Much of the music was vocal, and the text, usually sacred or devotional, was the source of the rhythm as well as of the melodic line. However, there were also liturgical dramas and other entertainment whose music was somewhat more complex, with instrumental accompaniment on bowed and/or plucked instruments, drums and pipes, and with two or more voice parts either singing together or in alternation. In the case of secular songs, the language was often vernacular and the subject matter far from liturgical. Purely instrumental music was also heard and danced to by the upper classes. Music was, like everything else for the Normans, something to be exported, imported and, perhaps most of all, assimilated.

115

55 *Highly ornate south doorway at Rochester Cathedral, Kent. The voussoirs above the doorway are typical of late Norman decorative sculpture, both in Britain and on the Continent*

Architecture

It was in the sphere of buildings and architecture that the Norman Conquest probably had its greatest impact. Cathedrals and abbeys were built, on a scale never seen before in Britain, in a continental Romanesque style, which, as time went on, absorbed Anglo-Saxon and Scandinavian elements to produce a distinctive Anglo-Norman Romanesque architecture. In the opinion of one leading authority, the Anglo-Norman school became 'perhaps the most advanced and progressive of all branches of northern Romanesque' (A.W. Clapham).

The Norman builders were so thorough in their reconstruction that there is virtually no pre-Conquest architecture surviving in any English cathedral or abbey above ground. The new 'Norman' architecture was used in thousands of parish churches built afresh throughout the country, as well as in the many small priories that Norman lords erected beside their manor houses or castles. Norman architecture was used on an equally lavish scale in secular buildings, not only in the great castles and palaces which sprang up, but also in vernacular town houses and a number of manor houses. Nothing on this scale of building had been seen since the Roman occupation of Britain and it was not repeated

56(a)   Unusual square Romanesque font from Norfolk

until the Victorian era. We are very fortunate to have a great wealth of eleventh- and twelfth-century architecture surviving in this country in England and Wales, but one has to take into account the rebuilding and destruction of Norman architecture over the last nine centuries to fully appreciate the Norman architectural revolution.

Norman Romanesque was introduced from the continent in the middle of the eleventh century. Its origins were in the classical and neo-classical buildings of northern Italy and Germany whose influence was transferred to Burgundy, notably the great abbey at Cluny, in the early eleventh century, and then brought to England by clerics such as William of Volpiano. It is true that Romanesque architecture had made its appearance in England prior to the Conquest at Edward the Confessor's Westminster Abbey (see **colour plate 11**) and possibly at Waltham Abbey which Harold, when Earl of Wessex, had started to build. The inspiration for Westminster Abbey appears to have come from Jumièges on the Seine, from whence also came Robert who became Edward's Archbishop of Canterbury (**52**). The massive ruins at Jumièges provide evidence of what Edward the Confessor's abbey, which 'he chose to have for himself as his place of burial there', looked like (see **colour plate 10**). Edward's church was rebuilt in the Gothic style in the thirteenth century and only small amounts of Norman work survive in the monastic buildings, although excavations earlier this century clearly demonstrated the structural affinity Westminster has with Jumièges.

In a survey which encompasses the history of Norman activity throughout Europe and Asia it is not possible to dwell too long on the details of Norman Romanesque. In essence,

56(b)   Primitive Romanesque font from St Mary's, Luppitt, Devon

Norman Romanesque architecture depended on the use of arcades of rounded arches. The main and most impressive arcade was surmounted by a second stage known as the triforium and that, in turn, carried a clear storey with a wall that could be pierced with windows. Anglo-Norman architecture was skilful in varying the proportions of these storeys. Blind arcading with pillar and arch construction against a blank wall was also a very popular form of decoration, samples of which can be seen at Gloucester cathedral (1089–1100), the chapter house at Worcester cathedral (pre-1125) and the chapter house at Wenlock priory (mid-twelfth century) (**53a** and **b**). One of the chief advantages of Norman Romanesque over earlier building designs was that it allowed the introduction of broader vaulting spans, enabling the construction of wider and higher buildings. Romanesque architects introduced other innovations, including the choir with an ambulatory and radiating chapels enclosing the eastern apse. This design was ideal for the display of shrines and relics and allowed the easy circulation of large numbers of pilgrims (**54**).

Anglo-Norman architecture also made a major contribution to the evolution of roof vaulting, which became an essential feature of later medieval architecture and led on to the development of Gothic. Indeed, Romanesque churches required very thick walls in order to carry the weight of stone vaulting, and it was the evolution of the pointed arch which enabled different methods of support to be introduced and, eventually, for piers and columns to replace the heavy walls.

Norman church architecture during the eleventh and twelfth centuries is barely discernible from military and vernacular stone architecture. It was characterised by the

*57(a) The elaborately
carved doorway
at Kilpeck
(Hereford and
Worcester) dating
from the mid-
twelfth century*

use of rounded arches, massive supports and heavy, solid walling and, for the most part, was plain, lacking elaborate decoration. Such decoration as there was tended to be in the Carolingian or sub-classical style, with little figurative carving. During the first half of the twelfth century there can be seen a clear fusion between Norman, Saxon and Viking motifs, both in decoration and in structural design. From about 1130, the flamboyant period of English Romanesque decorative carving began. The zig-zag chevron motif was central to this development and, during the twelfth century, became increasingly elaborate (**55**). From the later Norman period there are hundreds of surviving richly carved doorways, chancel arches, arcades, windows and fonts (**56a** and **b**). Norman Romanesque architecture derived its inspiration from many sources, including book illumination, goldsmiths' work, ivory carving and wooden sculpture. The fact that craftsmen were trained in several skills is demonstrated in an artists' manual, *Diversis Artigus c.*1100, which indicates that Anglo-Norman artists were proficient in a number of different artistic fields.

119

57(b)   Detail of grotesque mid twelfth-century carving from Kilpeck

Most aspects of Romanesque art and architecture were religious in character, but there were also secular images — often including crude or humorous images, some fantastic and grotesque — in the form of mythical animals. Twelfth-century Anglo-Norman capitals incorporated a wide range of designs and were sometimes extraordinarily ornate, with vivid sculptures of Biblical scenes and incidents from the lives of saints, but also incorporating symbols from everyday life and the signs of the zodiac.

There were marked regional variations in style and the work of distinctive schools of sculpture can be identified. One of the best known is that of the Herefordshire school, whose best surviving work can be see today at Kilpeck church (Herefords) (**57a** and **b**). There were other regional schools based on East Anglia and in the north. In the latter part of the twelfth century highly flamboyant Romanesque sculpture gave way to a more graceful, Gothic style imported from Burgundy by way of the Île de France and, in England, classified as early English, the date of its introduction corresponding neatly with the end of Norman rule.

7 The Normans in southern Europe

Even before the end of the tenth century the Norman presence in Europe was being felt well beyond the boundaries of the duchy. During the first half of the eleventh century contingents of Normans were to be found in Spain, Dalmatia and Asia Minor as well as Italy. The impetus for this mobility was partly pious, partly military, partly political, and in some cases a combination of all three. Normans were early participants in the pilgrimage to holy places, a movement that introduced them to Spain, Italy, Asia Minor and the Holy Land. Pilgrims from northern Europe were particularly interested in visiting places specifically associated with Christ, especially Jerusalem. Normans, along with others, stopped off at other significant religious sites including St Peter's in Rome and Mount Gargano in Apulia, a holy place since Roman times which had a shrine dedicated to the Archangel Michael. Pilgrims were often armed and travelled in groups for protection, making them virtually indistinguishable from mercenary knights, particularly as they often, of necessity, became involved in combat on their travels (**58**). The prowess of Norman knights meant that their services were in demand from an early date to help in the multitude of major and minor skirmishes in southern Europe, and it was in Italy that they found their most profitable arena.

In the tenth century Italy faced danger from several different directions. The peninsula was threatened by the Saracens of *Fraxinetum* (southern France), as well as those based around the estuary of the river Gariglianno which ran through Capua to the Tyrrhenian sea. It was reported by Liutbrand, Bishop of Cremona, that the Moslems of North Africa harried the coasts 'so that no-one coming from the west or north to make his prayers at the thresholds of the blessed apostles was able to get into Rome without either being taken prisoner by these men or only released on payment of a large ransom'. A joint expedition of Lombard, Greek and papal forces successfully extinguished the Saracen camps at the estuary of the river Garigliano in 915, and the base at *Fraxinetum* was finally destroyed in 973. However, the Saracen danger in southern Italy and the inability of local forces to dislodge them, particularly from their base in Sicily, provided a pretext for intervention by the Norman adventurers. In 982 the Emperor Otto II, marching south from Salerno, announced that he had come to 'defend the Christian population'. Although his campaign ended in disaster, as the young emperor died in Rome the following year after his army had been defeated in Torento, it paved the way for further incursions by northerners.

The growth in the popularity of pilgrimage to the shrine of St James of Compostela in the north-west of Spain in the tenth century eventually led to Frankish participation in the wars against the Spanish Moslems. As early as *c*.1020, a Norman, Roger de Tosney, is reported by one source to have engaged in cannibalism during a campaign against the Moslems in Spain, although knights from Burgundy and south-western France generally played a more prominent role in these battles than those from Normandy. In any case,

58   Carved capital with fighting knights, San Marcello Maggiore, Apulia

opportunities for Norman colonisation were strictly limited as the local Christian powers in re-conquered Spain strongly resisted any imperial ambitions from the north, as did the Byzantines in Asia Minor. In 1071, for instance, Roussel of Bailleul, who fought for Count Roger of Sicily before entering the service of the Greeks, appropriated a vast territory in Anatolia which was immediately reclaimed by the Byzantine emperor. A little earlier in 1065, Robert Crespin had organised an unsuccessful campaign in Spain in response to the 'detestable folly of the Saracens'. After an initial victory Crespin left a garrison in the city of Barbastro and returned north to gather a larger army to help resume the conquest, and presumably colonisation, in Spain. Amatus of Montecassino (1080), who chronicled Norman activity in the south, recounts that 'Christ was angered because the (Norman) knights gave themselves over to the love of fame. Therefore, because of their sins they lost what they had acquired and were chased out by the Saracens'.

The consequences of political developments in Normandy initiated by Duke Richard II contributed to the migration southwards. The political reforms he imposed resulted in a diminution of the authority of the lesser nobles who, as a result, periodically rebelled against ducal authority. These nobles, who incurred the duke's displeasure as a result of their rebellions, often migrated southwards. Increasingly also, the duke came to rely on the right of exile to deal with rebels and criminals; many who were thus expelled found their way south. Hugh Burnell, who killed the Countess Mabel of Bellême, fled with his brother to Italy in 1077, and thence to Constantinople; the brothers still did not feel safe from the duke, and went to live among the Saracens, 'studying their customs and languages', it is said. Refugees such as Abbot Robert of Grandmesnil and the monks of St Evroult, and William Werlerc, the former count of Mortain, escaped southwards to avoid a hostile political atmosphere at home. Others travelled south for gain; William of Montreuil, who went south *c*.1050, and William of Grandmesnil, who left Normandy *c*.1080, reaped enormous rewards. The latter was even able to marry a daughter of Robert Guiscard. Some were more circumspect about their migration; for instance, Hugh the Clerk, who set out in 1094, made arrangements in case he wanted to return home, and it is clear that many who travelled south later returned to Normandy.

One contemporary writer, Cloriclus, suggests that for the average Norman the Mediterranean lands were an Eldorado, and an examination of the names of those involved indicates that the largest number of those moving southwards in the eleventh century came from lower and middle-ranking families. Such analysis shows that the Normans were not alone and were accompanied by people from many other parts of France, particularly the north. Their strength was further increased in the south itself; a famous passage in the deeds of Robert Guiscard, written by William of Apulia, describes how 'the Normans . . . recruited Italians, taught them their language and instructed them in their customs'. The list of participants provided by Orderic Vitalis and reinforced by charter evidence would suggest that the main areas of emigration were from the extremely unstable regions in and beyond the southern marches of Normandy. It is clear from Orderic that a visit to southern Italy was an attractive prospect; the lure was such that it could even tempt nuns to renounce their vows and join members of their families who had already settled there. Orderic also tells the story of a cleric, Reginald Benedict, who twice made the journey from Normandy to southern Italy and back in order to raise funds from wealthy kinsmen.

The Normans in southern Italy

The Normans' most impressive political achievement in southern Europe was their political take-over of southern Italy and Sicily, which was accomplished in the face of opposition from the eastern empire of Byzantium, the western German empire, the Moslems and the Papacy (**59**). At the time the Normans appeared in the region, Italy lay on the border between east and west. The peninsula was divided into several small principalities which had various allegiances. Apulia and Calabria were under Byzantine occupation; in classical times southern Italy with Sicily had formed Magna Graecia, and at this time the area was still more Greek than Italian in spirit. The majority of its inhabitants spoke Greek and the churches and monasteries were Orthodox, under the Patriarch of Constantinople. Gaeta, Naples and Amalfi were small independent republics, while Benevento, Capua and Salerno were Lombard territories owing allegiance to the Holy Roman Empire based in Germany, and Sicily was in Arab hands (**60**).

Since early times Sicily had held a particular attraction for Greeks, and in the middle of the seventh century Syracuse had very briefly replaced Constantinople as the capital of the Eastern Empire. In the ninth century the Moslems, who for some time had been harassing the Byzantines who held the islands, saw their chance of achieving permanent occupation. When the Byzantine governor instigated a revolt proclaiming himself

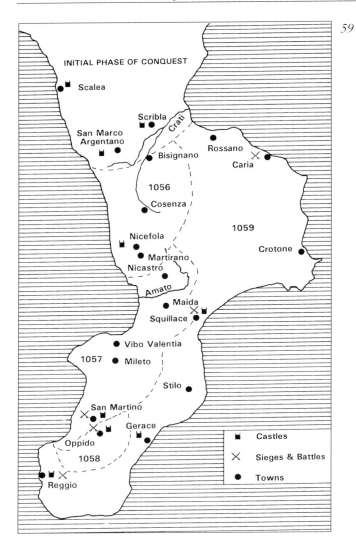

59 Map of southern Italy showing phases of Norman conquest

emperor he appealed to the Arabs for aid. In response they landed in strength and stormed Palermo, which they made their capital, and proceeded to conquer the island for themselves. After the fall of Syracuse in 878 the Byzantines admitted defeat, and all the other major cities on the island fell to the Moslems (**colour plate 23**). Palermo and the island as a whole prospered under Moslem rule, acting as an emporium for the rich trade with North Africa. Its cosmopolitan population consisted of merchants from throughout the Mediterranean including many from the maritime cities of Italy. New agricultural techniques were introduced under Arab rule, and luxuriant parks and gardens were planted in the Conca d'Oro, the area surrounding Palermo. Arab geographers record the draining of marshes, the cutting of irrigation channels and the cultivation of exotic vegetables, papyrus and sugar cane, the latter providing an important export commodity.

60   *Manuscript showing Arab army of the eleventh century*

The Arabs had also occupied parts of Apulia and Calabria and, although they had been more or less expelled from the mainland by 1000, a few pockets remained. These, together with their island stronghold of Sicily, presented a permanent threat to the Christian powers in Italy, as well as a constant source of embarrassment. It was into this environment that the Normans came with a crusading zeal, bringing with them all the dangers associated with the crusades to their fellow Christians.

Italy was too far from the centre of Byzantine control in Constantinople to defend itself adequately, either from the south or the north, and the fragmentation of political power in the peninsula added to Italy's vulnerability to conquest. Unlike the conquest of England, Norman rule in southern Italy was achieved on a piecemeal basis by mercenary soldiers in a process that lasted throughout the eleventh century. The Norman Roger de Hauteville, who became a count and then duke in Italy, had to first assert his authority amongst his compatriots, but finally, in 1130, his son Roger became a king, a position which had taken over a century to acquire. William the Conqueror, operating from a secure political base as duke of Normandy, had won the throne of England in less than four months after the Battle of Hastings.

The conquest of Italy was the work of individuals of relatively humble birth, many of them the younger sons of local lords for whom there was no room at home. Others were political exiles from Normandy, many of whom were impoverished on their arrival in Italy. Amatus provides a highly coloured description of the Normans riding gaily 'through the meadows and gardens — happy and joyful on their horses, cavorting hither and

125

thither'. Amatus adds that 'the citizens of the town of Venosa saw these unfamiliar knights and wondered at them and were afraid' and, one may add, not without reason! Amatus claimed that St Matthew appeared in a vision to the Archbishop of Salerno and had said

> It has been ordained in the presence of God that whosoever shall oppose the Normans will be put to flight by them; either they will all die or they will suffer great affliction. For this land has been given to the Normans by God, because of the perversity of those who used to hold it, the paternal ties that God has with the Normans, the just will of God turned the land over to them. For both the law of God and the law of the Empire command that the sons succeed to the patrimony of the fathers.

The revolts of Byzantine-held cities such as Bari against the representatives of a distant government, which itself was distracted by a long campaign in Bulgaria, and the internal dissent of Lombard princes amidst an ever-present threat of Moslem attack, provided a fertile field of activity for groups of Norman knights whose only loyalty lay to their own leaders. Accounts differ as to the date of the first appearance of Normans in southern Italy. Amatus recounted how a band of Norman pilgrims returning from Jerusalem 'before the year 1000' relieved Salerno from a siege by the Saracens, prompting prince Gaimar IV of Salerno to send to Normandy for more knights to serve him. Amongst those who responded to this invitation was one Gilbert who was wanted by Duke Robert I for killing a viscount and his brothers. According to other accounts a group of Norman émigrés joined a Lombard rebel called Mello *c*.1016. In this story Mello organised a campaign of harassment against the Greeks until his forces were decisively beaten at Callae in October 1018. The most reliable account reported that Norman knights were to be found south of the river Garigliano in 1017, firstly organised in small groups whose families were of little prominence in Normandy and who would fight for anyone who promised them a share of the booty. Thus the Normans did not operate as a coherent force; from time to time Normans fought each other on opposing sides and frequently employed Moslem and Byzantine troops in their own armies. Each Norman lord had his own interests to protect, but the Normans had not created this confusing situation which was to provide them with the opportunity for territorial expansion. Following Mello's flight to Germany the Normans split up, entering the service of the rulers of Salerno, Benevento, Capua and Montecassino. The first territory to fall into Norman hands was the town of Aversa where Gilbert's brother Rainulf gained control *c*.1030.

The House of Hauteville

To begin with, the early Norman adventurers succeeded in establishing themselves in southern Italy at the expense of local Byzantine overlords. It was a period of shifting loyalties and easy alliances, but the Normans were past-masters at pragmatic diplomacy and warfare. One of their early leaders was William of the Iron Arm, one of the sons of Tancred of Hauteville who came to Italy with his brother Drogo (*c*.1037). For the next century and a half it was the house of Hauteville (also known as the Tancredis) that was to dominate the politics of southern Italy and Sicily. The Hautevilles originated in a small, unprepossessing village called Hauteville-la-Guichard, which lies some eight miles to the north-east of Coutances in the Cotentin peninsula of Normandy (**colour plate 25**). Tancred was a minor provincial baron, commander of a modest group of 10 knights in the service of Duke Robert II. Little is known of him apart except that he fathered five sons by his first wife (Muriella) and a further seven sons and at least three daughters by the second (Frendesendis). His small family fief was clearly inadequate for his large numbers of dependants, and the opportunities offered to a steady stream of Hauteville sons in southern Italy were enticing. The three oldest Hauteville sons — William, Drogo and Humphrey — attached themselves to Rainulf's army at Aversa. Significantly, the Hautevilles were part of a Norman force that joined a large Byzantine expedition to attack Sicily in 1038. To begin with the Greek army, under the leadership of general Maniakes and including a Scandinavian element as well as the Normans, was successful. By 1040 the eastern half of Sicily had been restored to Christian hands. However, after a notable victory at Syracuse a dispute broke out between the Byzantines and Normans; the latter claimed that they had not received their fair share of plunder from the captured city and returned to mainland Italy. This desertion, compounded by the loss of the Byzantine leader who was recalled to Constantinople about another matter, left the Greek army thoroughly demoralised, and the Sicilian campaign collapsed as a result.

In 1042 Maniakes, who had returned as governor of southern Italy, fell out of favour with the emperor once more, was himself proclaimed emperor by his troops, and crossed the Adriatic to march on Constantinople. He met and defeated an imperial army at Ostrovo in Bulgaria, but died during the battle. His head was carried back to Constantinople and impaled on a spear for exhibition in the Hippodrome. Maniakes had taken with him a number of Norman mercenaries who, after his death, entered the service of the Greek Empire. They were the nucleus of the Norman force which was then formed in Byzantium; a force periodically swelled by the arrival of other adventurers from Italy. Eventually Normans were chosen for some of the highest offices at court, one of them being Roussel de Bailleul who for 40 years intrigued and fought in the Byzantine world, and who at one stage almost succeeded in mounting the throne of Constantinople.

In the meantime in Italy, the Hautevilles themselves turned against their erstwhile employers, the Byzantines, and inflicted a series of defeats upon them. Nevertheless, at this stage some semblance of loyalty to local rulers still remained. William de Hauteville was elected Norman count in 1042, accepting the Lombard prince Gaimar of Salerno as his overlord, and Robert Guiscard (his half-brother) married the Lombard princess Sichelgaita. But the Norman skill of benefiting from rival claims to authority soon manifested itself. At an assembly held at Capua in 1047 in the presence of the emperor Henry III, Norman claims to rights and possessions in the south were confirmed. This meeting essentially recognised the territorial acquisitions of the Normans and implicitly accepted that they would acquire more in due course. When William died in 1048 his brother Drogo succeeded as leader of the Apulian Normans.

After Drogo was killed in 1051 Robert Guiscard (nicknamed 'crafty'), probably the most energetic of the Hautevilles, became Norman leader. Although he concentrated his activities on mainland politics, he did play a role in the conquest of Sicily as well as in

Norman campaigns in the eastern Mediterranean. Robert Guiscard's early career was one of unabashed brigandage; it is recorded that he 'shrank from no violence and nothing was sacred to him; he respected neither old age, nor women and children and on occasion he spared neither church nor monastery'. The Normans continued to spread and eventually, fearful of their growing power, Pope Leo IX, in alliance with the Byzantines and Swabians in the employ of the Holy Roman Emperor, was provoked into taking up arms against them. He was defeated at the battle of Civitate (1053), fought on the banks of the river Fortore, where he found himself with a large but badly trained and equipped army facing the Norman enemy. Before the battle the German troops had urged the Pope to, 'Command the Normans to leave Italy, to lay down their arms here and to return to the land whence they came'. In the event it was the Swabians who were killed to the last man. Pope Leo watched the battle from the ramparts of Civitate and saw half his army put to flight and the other half remorselessly butchered. After this devastating defeat Leo was captured by the Normans and kept in detention near Bari for nine months.

Nevertheless, by the end of the decade Robert Guiscard had emerged as a defender of papal interests in the south and was acting as a counterpoise to the German Holy Roman Emperor. In 1057 Robert threatened Reggio, the gateway to Sicily, but yet another Hauteville brother, Roger, had arrived in Italy and had established his headquarters at Monteleone. To begin with Robert and Roger quarrelled and Roger took up a career of brigandage during which it was largely his brother's territory that suffered. Robert Guiscard eventually made peace with Roger and as settlement gave him half of Calabria. In 1059 the Normans were once again reconciled with the papacy in the form of Pope Nicholas II, who in August 1059 summoned the Council of Melfi as part of an attempt to reduce papal dependence on the Holy Roman emperor, but also in response to the Norman threat to the vassal states of the papacy. At the Council, which effectively gave the Normans in southern Italy respectability, Nicholas received homage and the promise of military aid from Robert Guiscard and Richard of Capua which he used to enter Rome and remove the anti-Pope Benedict X. In return, Nicholas recognised Robert as duke of Apulia, Calabria and in the future of Sicily, and Richard as Prince of Capua (**61**). With this papal recognition and encouragement the Normans continued their conquest in south Italy so that by 1060 the Byzantines had effectively been reduced to holding only their capital Bari and a few coastal ports, but they were still not beaten.

The siege of Bari

In 1060 Roger and Robert Guiscard took Taranto, Brindisi and Reggio from the Byzantines. With the occupation of Reggio, 'he and his brother Roger' it is said 'were irresistibly attracted to Sicily'; but the Byzantine challenge to their rear in Apulia remained. Between 1060 and 1071 Guiscard remained locked in the struggle with the Byzantines, a struggle from which he emerged successful, but, as a result of this preoccupation with the Byzantines, his role in the conquest of Sicily was secondary to that of his brother, Roger.

Throughout the 1060s, Robert Guiscard was in constant conflict with the Byzantines in southern Italy, and by a war of attrition he gradually pushed back the territory under

61   *Norman church at Molfetta, Apulia*

62   The Norman church at Bari

Byzantine control. In 1068 Guiscard was victorious in Lechia, Gravina and Obbiano, and in the summer of the same year he lay siege to the last Byzantine stronghold, Bari (**62**). As supplies reached the city by sea, it was able to hold out for three years. He encircled the promontory of the old city with a barricade of boats, all chained one to the other. With his army surrounding the city on land he had achieved a complete blockade, making it even more surprising that the citizens held out for the incredible length of time that they did. Finally, the Norman fleet overcame the Byzantine ships which were bringing reinforcements outside the blockade, and the inhabitants entered into negotiations with Guiscard and surrendered the town in April 1071. The capture of Bari marked the real end of Byzantine power in Italy. Moreover, it brought Guiscard a major advantage, ensuring a fortified port of the first rank in the very heart of Apulia, which assisted him greatly in maintaining his authority and also provided him with a base from which to look eastwards.

Relations between the Normans and the papacy were often strained, and in March 1074 Guiscard and the Normans were excommunicated by Pope Gregory VII. Cencius, the leader of the aristocracy in Rome which was hostile to the Pope, now offered to make Guiscard emperor if he would help them to expel Gregory VII. But Guiscard recognised the dangers of accepting such a proposal and established an alliance between the Normans, including the forces of his one-time enemy, Richard of Capua, and Greek and Norman contingents. This created a formidable Norman force, which went on to besiege Salerno and Naples.

In May 1076 Robert Guiscard laid siege to Salerno, assisted by Greek and Moslem contingents in his own army and by the forces of Richard of Capua. The besieging army finally succeeded in overcoming the resistance of Salerno's weakened citizens and Robert entered the city on 10 December 1076. At one point at the siege of the citadel a stone hurled from the tower seriously injured Robert, but he recovered. At the Council of Rome in March 1078, the Pope once more excommunicated 'those Romans who attacked the territory of St Peter (i.e. the March of Fermo and the Duchy of Spoleto), those who besieged Benevento and dared to lay waste the campagnia, the Marittima, and the Sabina', forbidding any bishop or priest to allow Normans to attend divine offices. Following the successful suppression of a revolt which extended over large areas of Guiscard's territory, the Duke of Apulia at last came to an agreement with the Pope at Ceprano on 29 June 1080.

Robert's relationship with the papacy remained stormy but, during the final political crisis of Hildebrand's pontificate, Robert intervened on the Pope's behalf against the Emperor Henry IV. This intervention manifested itself in a savage attack on Rome by Norman troops in 1084 and forced the withdrawal of the Pope, under Norman protection, to Salerno (where he died in 1085).

The mercenary Normans of southern Italy probably operated in a manner not too distant from their Scandinavian forebears, at least during the initial phase of conquest, but unlike the Scandinavians the Normans brought few settlers with them. They came to represent a ruling élite above peasants, administrators and clergy — Lombard, Byzantine and Moslem — who retained their customs and laws. The first generations of Norman settlers assimilated the political and cultural heritage of the regions they conquered and this was a policy they were to adopt throughout their time in the south (**63**).

The Normans in the Adriatic

Guiscard had long seen Constantinople as an attainable goal and, for their part, the Byzantine Emperors could not ignore their powerful neighbour and sought his alliance from time to time. About 1075, negotiations with the Byzantines resulted in the betrothal of one of Guiscard's daughters to the young son of the emperor, Michael VII. However, Michael was peaceably dethroned in 1078 (he went on to become Archbishop of Ephesus), meaning that the Norman alliance collapsed and Guiscard's daughter, Helena, was sent to a convent before she could marry the young prince. The projected marriage served as a pretext for a declaration of war by Guiscard when, in 1080, he determined to profit by the disturbances that had broken out in the Greek Empire and attempted to seize Constantinople. Under the pretext of defending his daughter's rights, the Duke of Apulia became the champion of the dethroned emperor and started to assemble a force to attack Constantinople. As his plans aroused only moderate enthusiasm amongst his vassals, Guiscard carried out a fraud and, in the middle of 1080, he presented a bogus Greek Orthodox monk named Rector as the real Michael VII, said to have escaped from a monastery where he had been imprisoned by his successor. By this device the Norman leader hoped to enthuse his vassals and conciliate the Greek population.

63 *Norman chessman from southern Italy, showing chain mail, round shield and broad sword*

Pope Gregory VII agreed to support Guiscard, who persuaded him that the proposed expedition would represent a crusade against the increasingly remote Eastern church. This had been close to the Pope's heart for a number of years and would end the schism between Eastern and Western Christianity, thus bringing about a reunion with the Greek Church. In July 1080 the Pope wrote to the bishops of Apulia and Calabria encouraging them to support the duke's plans. At the end of May 1081 Guiscard took the initiative and landed at Valona, which had already been taken by his son, Bohemond, along with a number of other ports in the eastern Adriatic. Soon, the island of Corfu fell into Norman hands, after which they laid siege to Durazzo — the old Roman Dyrrachium — capital and chief port of Illyria, from which the Roman Via Egnatia ran eastwards across the Balkan peninsula, through Macedonia, Thrace and thence to Constantinople. Initially the Normans suffered a setback at sea at the hands of the Venetians, whom Alexius

Comnenus had summoned to his aid. The Venetians used several devices against the Normans including, apparently, the old Byzantine practice of Greek fire. The Norman chronicler, Geoffrey Malaterra, records how 'they blew that fire, which is called Greek fire and is not extinguished by water, through submerged pipes, and thus cunningly burned one of our ships under the very waves of the sea'. The Normans nevertheless continued the siege of the Illyrian capital, and on 18 October 1081 they defeated a Byzantine army which contained a significant English contingent and which the emperor had brought to relieve the besieged city. Finally, on 21 February 1082, Durazzo was taken.

In the spring of 1082 Guiscard was obliged to return to Apulia. Pope Gregory VII had sent him urgent appeals for help, threatened as he was by the Emperor Henry IV's expedition to Italy. In addition, the new Byzantine emperor, Alexius Comnenus, was subsidising the German king and, at the same time, Abelard and Herman, Robert Guiscard's nephews, had launched a successful insurrection in Apulia. Leaving Bohemond to continue the war against the Byzantines, Guiscard returned to Italy where he spent time in 1082–3 re-establishing his authority in Apulia. In May 1084 he marched on Rome, which by that time was occupied by the German emperor. Henry did not wait for the Normans to arrive before departing, but his retreat did not prevent Guiscard from entering the city in force; he sacked Rome and freed Gregory VII, whom the partisans of the anti-Pope, Clement III, were besieging. As soon as the Pope was free, Guiscard sent him to Salerno for safety and immediately returned to his task of conquering Constantinople. The sack of Rome by the Normans, with the help of Arab contingents, was as brutal an attack as that troubled city had ever experienced.

Churches, palaces, ancient temples came crashing down before the advancing flames. The Capitol and the Palatine were gutted; in the whole area between the Colosseum and the Lateran hardly a single building escaped the inferno. Many of the inhabitants perished in their dwellings; others fleeing for their lives were cut down by the Normans as they ran, or else were captured and sold into slavery.

After his father had departed Bohemond again defeated the Greeks, at Yanina and Arta. He then occupied Ochrid, Veria, Servia, Vodena, Moglena, Pelagonia, Tzibikon and Trikala, but in 1083 he, in return, was defeated outside Larissa by Alexius Comnenus and was shortly afterwards obliged to return to Italy in order to raise money to pay his troops. After this setback to Bohemond the Byzantines regained the advantage and the Normans lost all the territory that they had conquered, including Durazzo. Consequently, when Guiscard took the field in the autumn of 1084, he had no foothold on the eastern side of the Adriatic. While his son Roger Borsa occupied Avlona, the duke himself proceeded to Butrinto and in November he was once again at Corfu. Guiscard was twice defeated near Cassiope by the Venetian fleet, but he took his revenge when he won an overwhelming victory near Corfu town, which fell into his hands as a result of this success. He sent his army to winter on the banks of the Glycys while he took himself to Bundicia. During the winter an epidemic of cholera decimated the Norman army. Nevertheless, hostilities were resumed at the beginning of the summer, and Roger set out to attack the island of Cephalonia. On the way to join his son, Guiscard fell ill. He was obliged to stop at Arta where he died on 17 July 1085, in the presence of his wife Sichelgaita and his son Roger. Although the Guiscard had built a magnificent new cathedral in Sicilian Norman style dedicated to St Matthew in Salerno (**64**), he had expressly asked to be buried with his

64   The cloisters of Salerno Cathedral, built by Robert Guiscard

brothers in the abbey church of the Santissima Trinità at Venosa. His epitaph read, 'Here lies Guiscard, terror of the world.' With Guiscard's death the heroic era of the history of the Normans in the south drew to a close. Bohemond turned his energies and attention to the crusades, and his immediate successors were unable to maintain his authority in the east. They abandoned his plans for the conquest of the empire, which were only revived when the counts of Sicily became monarchs and were able to consolidate his imperial work for a while.

The First Crusade

The Normans had been unofficial crusaders of a kind for the best part of a century when the western church embarked upon the Crusades to reclaim the Holy Land. The First Crusade was proclaimed by Pope Urban II at Clermont Ferand in the Central Massif of France, on 27 November 1095. This followed on from a request for military aid against the Moslems of Asia Minor by the Byzantine Emperor Alexius I Comnenus. Pope Urban II launched the crusade with the intention not only of helping the Byzantines, but also of recapturing Jerusalem for Christianity, whilst simultaneously channelling the troublesome and war-like knightly classes (many of them Frankish) into a useful campaign outside Europe. The Pope called for liberation of the east, the eastern churches and the holy places from oppression and defilement from unbelievers, and his passionate appeal was greeted by shouts of *deus levault* — 'God wills it'.

The First Crusade was primarily a Frankish affair involving Normans both from the duchy and from southern Italy, although the Sicilian Normans did not participate. Such was the Frankish dominance of the crusade that the Saracens and Byzantines called all the westerners Franks. The prominent Normans who participated included Robert Curthose, Duke of Normandy, who provided two armies numbering, perhaps, 1000 knights, plus infantry. He was joined by Stephen Henry, Count of Blois, who was the Conqueror's son-in-law through his marriage to Adela and Robert, Count of Flanders, each with, respectively, 300 and 600 knights plus infantry. Among the other Norman and Anglo-Norman lords to join Duke Robert were veterans of the Battle of Hastings, most notably the roguish Odo, Bishop of Bayeux, the Conqueror's half-brother; he did not reach the Levant as he died in Palermo, where he was buried in 1097; Ralph Guadar, the Earl of Norfolk, who had been exiled from England since 1075, William de Courcy, and the one-time pretender to the English throne, Edgar the Atheling. This army travelled to the Levant via Norman Italy, where they passed the winter of 1096–7 with Roger Borsa, now Duke of Apulia and Calabria. The second of the two Norman contingents was drawn from Norman Italy itself, under the leadership of Bohemond. This was a small but effective army consisting of about 500 knights, amongst whom were many members of leading Norman Italian families including the Hautevilles(**65**).

In 1097 the crusader army travelled from Constantinople across Asia Minor, captured Nicaea from the Turks, and then achieved a significant victory over the Turks at the battle of Dorylaeum. They then made their way by various routes to Antioch in the Levant, which was reached on 20 October 1097 after an appalling journey in autumn rains across the Anatolian Mountains. A further seven months passed before the crusaders eventually

BELLVM INTER COROHRAM ET FRANC

65   Frankish and Muslem armies during the first crusade

entered Antioch on 3 June 1098, after which they were themselves besieged inside the walls. The siege of Antioch involved two major battles, both of which the Christians won, and established Bohemond as the outstanding military leader of the first crusade (**66**). When the Latin armies moved on towards Jerusalem in 1099 Bohemond, with most of his Italian Normans, stayed behind, adopting the title of Prince of Antioch and establishing the furthest flung territory of the disparate Norman 'empire'.

Raymond IV, Count of Toulouse, who had been the first prince to respond to Urban II's call to crusade in the Holy Land, argued that Antioch should be given to the Byzantine Emperor. However, Bohemond I claimed it for himself and expelled Raymond's garrison. Thereafter, Raymond appears as the leader of the crusade, arranging the march to Jerusalem and playing a crucial role in the storming of that city in 1099.

66   *Manuscripts showing the siege of Antioch*

Antioch

Antioch had been an essential objective for the crusaders as it was a See of St Peter, and formerly a great Christian centre, as well as being the gateway to the Holy Land from Asia Minor. It was also heavily defended. The medieval city has now almost vanished, save for the outline of its defences, but it is said that there were 360 towers along its walls with five gates and posterns and a powerful citadel on the south side (**67a** and **b**). The Anglo-Norman contingent continued on to Jerusalem where they participated with distinction in the siege and capture of the city on 15 July 1099, but within a few months Duke Robert of Normandy, with the remnants of his army, left Jerusalem for home.

*67(a) Engraving of Antioch in the eighteenth century; only the city wall circuit with bastions
survives from the Norman period*

The Crusade had greatly enhanced Robert's reputation, and on the way home he
stopped in southern Italy where he married indirectly into the Hauteville dynasty. His
new wife was Sibyl, the daughter of the Count of Conversana, who was himself Robert
Guiscard's nephew. Although Norman involvement in Jerusalem continued, it was
Antioch which was to be the most permanent legacy of the Norman involvement in the
first crusade. In 1104 the Byzantine emperor Alexius Comnenus, who claimed Antioch as
a fief of the empire, sacked Bohemond's territories. In 1105, faced with pressures from
Saracens, Greeks and Franks, Bohemond travelled to France in search of reinforcements.
There he married King Philip's daughter, Constance, and managed to raise a new army,
which unwisely he directed towards Constantinople. He was defeated by an alliance of
Byzantines and Venetians in the Balkans, and he was forced to seek terms under which the
Normans were allowed to remain in Antioch but under Byzantine overlordship.
Bohemond never returned to the east and died in Apulia in 1111, where he was buried at
the cathedral of Canosa. His curiously oriental-looking mausoleum sits outside the south
wall of the church — the earliest surviving Norman tomb in southern Italy (**68**).

Throughout the twelfth century the Byzantine emperors remained closely involved in
the affairs of Antioch. In 1136 as part of a campaign against the Normans of Sicily, the
emperor John Comnenus besieged Antioch (**69**). The Prince of Antioch, Raymond of
Poitiers, was forced to capitulate and recognise the emperor as his overlord. Relations
between the Byzantines and Normans were, however, far from easy, and in 1144 John's son

67(b)   Coins of Bohemond I, King of Antioch

Manuel Comnenus devastated the principality and it was only the fall of the neighbouring crusader state of Edessa that prevented a total Byzantine takeover. Thereafter Antioch formed a Frankish stronghold in the face of an ever-present Muslim threat.

The conquest and establishment of Antioch between 1098 and 1119 was an exercise and demonstration of *Norminitas*. It was, above all, a characteristic example of aristocratic colonisation. Antioch became the centre of the Norman-controlled principalities in the Holy Land. Under its first two princes Bohemond (1098–1111) and Roger (1112–19), the state of Antioch came to occupy the whole of the region between Cicilia in the north and central Syria in the south. When Jerusalem fell to Saladin in 1187 Antioch survived as a Latin stronghold, and remained so until it was eventually captured by Moslem forces in 1268; as such it was the longest surviving of all 'Norman' territories. The new Frankish nobility in Antioch, almost exclusively Normans from Italy, displaced or subdued their Moslem predecessors while being heavily outnumbered by the indigenous population. As in Italy they were able to take advantage of pre-existing divisions between Moslems and resident Christians. Nevertheless, by comparison with the occupation of Edessa, where there was an almost peaceful take-over by Baldwin of Boulogne and his few followers, in the establishment of the principality of Antioch there was hard fighting against entrenched Moslem lords and against a resurgent Byzantium. The result was a thinly dispersed military aristocracy, essentially alien in spite of fraternisation and occasional social contacts. The principality was held together by a sense of identity and kinship and by the bonds of feudal loyalties, service and obligation. The aristocracy was not only military, but also mounted. This alien military and mounted aristocracy could never become integrated with native society, as the Normans in England and southern Italy were eventually to do. As it was, rent collection from surrounding peasantry often proved to be a military expedition in its own right. The Norman aristocracy lived in castles that dominated the

68   Bohemond's elaborate tomb, Canosa, Apulia

countryside and acted as centres for their lordships. It is appropriate that the best-known surviving artefacts of crusading history remain the crusader castles which were used to control regions with a maximum economy of manpower.

One of the most difficult jobs for the Normans was the Latinisation of the church in Antioch, which was achieved only in the face of fierce opposition from the Byzantine church. As opportunities arose, Latin bishops were appointed and the patriarch of Antioch reconstructed and reformed the church on Latin lines. Also, monasticism played a fundamental role in the westernisation of the church in the form of the foundation of great Benedictine abbeys, St Paul, St George and St Simian, where western monks replaced their Greek Orthodox brothers. Similarly, the advent of the military orders, most notably the Templars and Hospitallers and their rise in fortune from the mid-twelfth century onwards which led to their domination of the religious and political affairs of Antioch, was a major feature of the Norman territory. Most of the buildings

69   *The Byzantine Emperor John Comnenus, who opposed Norman Sicilian expansion in the mid-twelfth century*

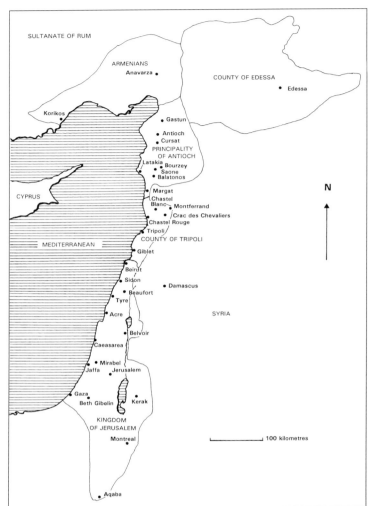

70 *Map of Antioch
and the crusader
kingdoms*

associated with this take-over of the church have disappeared. It is, therefore, in the great castle ruins that we are able to identify the Norman hand in places such as Baghras, Bourzay, Margat and Soane. In the succeeding century Antioch become increasingly eastern in character, although recent research has suggested that its Norman rulers maintained a distinct, albeit Frankish identity (**70**). The crusader cities also had merchant communities from north Italy, notably Venice, Genoa and Pisa as well as representatives of the Knights Templar and Hospitallers. It was the last of all Norman principalities to fall when it was brutally sacked by the Moslem armies of the Egyptian sultan Baybar I in 1268. The fall of Antioch and of Jaffa in the same year marked the beginning of the end of Frankish rule in the Levant.

The Second and Third Crusades

The Second Crusade was declared after the capture of the crusader state of Edessa in 1144. Louis VII of France led the crusade, which turned out to be an unmitigated disaster. As in the first crusade the Sicilian Normans did not participate directly, largely because of the prominent role still played by Moslems in government. By this time the remainder of southern Italy was under the control of King Roger, so there was no equivalent to Bohemond from Apulia to follow the cross. Roger did, perhaps disingenuously, offer to transport the crusaders to the Holy Land. When this offer was turned down he planned a campaign in the eastern Mediterranean, under the leadership of George of Antioch (**71**), which was interpreted by Byzantine chroniclers as a betrayal of Christianity and which brought the German and Byzantine emperors and the Venetians into an alliance against the Norman Italians.

In the autumn of 1147 the Normans sailed from Otranto, capturing Corfu without a struggle. They then rounded the Peloponnese, leaving detachments at strategic positions along the coast, and sailed up the eastern coast to Euboea. It then appears that there was an attack on Athens, after which George retraced his steps, but not before attacking the Ionian islands and ravaging the coastal towns of the Gulf of Corinth. His progress, Choniates Nicetas wrote, was 'like a sea monster, swallowing everything in its path'.

Of the raiding parties that George sent ashore, one penetrated the hinterland as far as Thebes, centre of Byzantine silk manufacture. In addition to plundering large quantities of silk, the admiral captured a large number of Jewish women silk workers who were transported to the Tiraz palace workshop in Palermo. From Thebes, the raiders moved on to Corinth where they pillaged the city and carried off the relics of St Theodore. By this time, wrote20 Nicetas, 'the Sicilian vessels were so low in the water with the weight of their plunder that they seemed more like merchantmen than the pirate ships they really were'.

In 1149 the Byzantines recaptured Corfu, but George of Antioch, Emir of Emirs, took a fleet of 40 ships up the Hellespont and over the Marmara Sea to the walls of Constantinople. After an unsuccessful attempt at landing the Sicilians had raided some distance up the Bosphorous, pillaging the rich villas along the Adriatic shore in the way that their Viking forbears would have recognised and applauded. This campaign in the eastern Mediterranean marked the end of Roger's overseas adventures. It managed to upset virtually all the major Christian powers, but it may have successfully delayed any concentrated attack on the Norman kingdom. Within five years both George of Antioch and King Roger were dead, and this significant phase of Norman expansionism was over.

King William II re-launched Norman expansionism in 1174 with an expedition against Saladin in Egypt. This, however, was undertaken as part of an alliance, and its failure meant that there were no further significant Norman campaigns from Sicily until those in 1180 and 1182 in the Balearics, which had become a favourite target for Norman raids during the final decades of their rule in Sicily.

In June 1185 a large Sicilian fleet, under the command of William II's cousin Tancred of Leche, sailed from Messina. Once again it was Durazzo, Byzantine's largest port in the Adriatic, which fell to them first. After a rapid march across the Balkans, by 6 August the Norman army was encamped outside the walls of Thessalonica, while on the 15th the

71   *George of Antioch prostrate before the Virgin Mary, mosaic from the Martorana church, Palermo*

fleet, having sailed round the Peloponnese, established a blockade in the harbour, marking the beginning of the siege. On 24 August, from both sides simultaneously, the Sicilian troops poured into the second city of the Byzantine Empire and sacked it, massacring the population. It was one of the worst recorded outrages in Norman history. Nicetas writes

> These barbarians carried their violences to the very foot of the altars in the presence of the holy images . . . it was thought strange that they should wish to destroy our icons, using them as fuel for the fires on which they cooked. More criminal still, they would dance upon the altars, before which the angels themselves trembled, and sing profane songs, then they would piss all over the church, flooding the floors with urine.

The Normans moved eastwards, and when their fleet was already in the Marmara, awaiting the army's arrival which was imminent, the Sicilians were attacked, defeated and Thessalonica restored to Byzantine rule, leaving the battered army to return to Italy across the Balkans. The Sicilian navy was intact, however, and on its return home attacked Cyprus. In the desultory struggle that followed we first hear of the fleet's new commander, Margaritus of Brindisi, the last great admiral of Norman Sicily.

In the autumn of 1187 Margaritus was summoned back to Sicily and ordered to re-fit his ships in haste and then to sail as early as possible for the Holy Land. On Friday 2 October Moslem armies under Saladin had taken Jerusalem, prompting the launch of the third crusade. This time there was no hesitation about Sicilian involvement. Indeed, in the vanguard William II alone of European monarchs had a contingent already in the field. The Sicilian fleet consisted of ships and 200 knights, but through 1188 and 1189, for most of the time, they represented virtually the only organised resistance to the Saracens. Margaritas kept up a steady patrol of the coast, blocking Saladin's forces on a number of occasions. In July 1188 news of the admiral's arrival off Tripolis caused Saladin to raise the siege of Krak des Chevaliers, but on 18 November 1189 King William II died, marking the beginning of the short epilogue to Norman rule in southern Italy.

Henry II of England had died in the same year and was succeeded by Richard I who became the effective leader of the crusade. Both King Philip Augustus of France and Richard I arrived in Messina in September 1190. His sister Joanna had been married to William II. Within two weeks Richard had captured and sacked Messina, the second city of the island. After wintering in Messina Richard came to an accommodation with Tancred, the new Sicilian king, and they exchanged gifts; five galleys and four horse transports for Richard and for Tancred King Arthur's sword, Excalibur itself, which had been found only a few weeks before lying beside the old king's body at Glastonbury — a curious and highly unlikely story.

Eventually, in early spring of 1191, both King Philip and King Richard sailed for the Holy Land. The English fleet returned in 1194, together with those of the Pisans and Genoese. They were supporting the claim of the emperor Henry VI to the crown of the 'Two Sicilies'. Richard himself had jut been released from captivity by one of Henry's vassals in Germany and part of his ransom was to help the emperor obtain the crown.

The Normans in North Africa

Given Sicily's vital strategic location in the centre of the Mediterranean it is perhaps hardly surprising that the Normans also gained territories in North Africa. George of Antioch was the principal architect of Roger II's North African empire. In 1146 he captured Tripoli, marking the culmination of a dozen years of regular raids and minor conquests along the coast. This victory had given Roger control of the entire coastline as far as Tunis, but the Normans were not interested in political domination in this case, they were far more concerned with the economic and strategic advantages to be gained from possessions on the southern coast of the Mediterranean. Commercially, by occupying the main ports he would be able to eliminate middle-men; in particular installing the king's agents to lead the great caravans that penetrated southwards. Strategically, the aim was to command the narrow sea between Sicily and Tunis which, in effect, meant domination of the central Mediterranean.

As always, the politics of the twelfth-century world were not straightforward. Following a rift with Prince Hassan of Mahdiyya, George of Antioch led a fleet of 250 ships against the port in 1148. George of Antioch's death in 1153 saw the end of Sicilian expansion in North Africa. Hardly had the Norman presence in North Africa been established than it started to disintegrate. In February 1156 the population of Sfax massacred every Christian within the city. In 1158 the islands of Djerba and Kerkinna off the coast of Tunisia revolted, which was the signal for Tripoli itself to rise up against the Normans. By the middle of 1159 only Mahdiyya was left in Sicilian hands. Those remaining Christians from the North African empire flocked to the city and such were the numbers that arrived that a new archbishop was installed to minister to them. The Moslems were intent on eradicating the last traces of Christian domination from their continent. On 20 July, with the city surrounded on all sides, the siege of Mahdiyya began. A fleet was sent to relieve the city, but for reasons unknown it failed to engage the enemy and returned to Italy. There was no further help from Palermo, and on 11 January 1160 Mahdiyya surrendered. The garrison was given safe conduct, and returned with arms and baggage, back to Sicily.

The loss of the North African empire was blamed on William I and his chief minister Maio who, it was believed, had let the territories go too readily. The charitable and generally accepted view is that William had enough on his agenda without becoming involved in a protracted rearguard action in North Africa. He was still in conflict with the German and Byzantine empires, as well as the papacy and an endless number of independent and semi-independent states, to say nothing of an endemic revolutionary situation within his own borders. He may well have calculated that to take on the might of the Almohads was one enemy too many.

The Norman kings had struggled against immense odds to gain their kingdom in Sicily and southern Italy. The 'Two Sicilies' had become a major power in the Mediterranean, able to control trade and commerce and make a significant contribution in military affairs. But the Norman kingdom had few natural friends and, in some respects, everybody's natural enemy. After it was established it was obliged to keep fighting for its survival at home, with constant threats from outside. It was never allowed an extended period of peace during which it could have built up its wealth and resources to the point where it could have achieved its aim of becoming the true master of the Mediterranean.

8 The Norman Kingdom of Sicily

The Conquest of Sicily (72)

At the same time that the Normans were involved in campaigns both in southern Italy and the Balkans, they were also intent on winning back Sicily to the Christian world. The richness and fertility of Sicily were renowned and clearly attracted the Normans, while the presence of Moslems in Sicily must have appeared to them as posing a constant threat to their newly acquired Italian possessions (**colour plate 27**). Malaterra wrote

> . . . hearing about infidel Sicily, and observing it was on the other side of that very narrow strip of water, Roger, who was always avid for dominion, was seized by ambition to acquire it, thinking that it would be of benefit both to his soul and indeed to his body if he could restore that land which had been surrendered to idols, to divine worship and dispose of it in service to God, and take temporal possession of the fruit and produce of the land which that people, disagreeable to God, has usurped from themselves.

According to Malaterra, Robert and Roger were planning their Sicilian campaign even before they had secured Reggio and before Roger had even been on a reconnaissance mission to Messina. In February 1061 Roger allied himself with the Emir of Syracuse and Catania, Ibn Thimna, who sought to enlist Roger's aid against his rival Ibn Hawwas Enis of Castrogiovanni and Agrigento. Roger spent March and April preparing for an invasion, and the following month Robert Guiscard arrived in Reggio with reinforcements, but a Moslem fleet despatched from Palermo prevented the Norman fleet from crossing. Robert remained behind with the bulk of the Norman army, acting as a decoy, while Roger crossed the straits with a much smaller force which managed to surprise and capture the practically undefended town of Messina. The Moslem fleet retreated to Palermo allowing Robert to follow Roger to Messina with the remainder of the Norman forces. The two Normans, Robert and Roger, spent the rest of the year campaigning in Sicily, but apart from taking the town of Troina were unable to secure a firm foothold on the island.

The following spring (1062) Roger and Ibn Thimna successfully besieged Petralia, some 30 miles east of Troina, but later that season, after Roger had returned to Calabria, his Moslem ally was ambushed and killed. When Roger returned to Sicily in midsummer 1062, he went to Troina and found to his relief that, despite the retreat of the Norman garrison there, the Moslems had not reoccupied the city. But in the process of re-establishing the garrison Roger alienated the local Greek Christian population. They claimed, probably with justification, that his troops had violated their womenfolk and responded by rebelling; with the help of Moslem forces from a nearby fortress, they besieged the count, his wife and his men for four months before Norman control was restored.

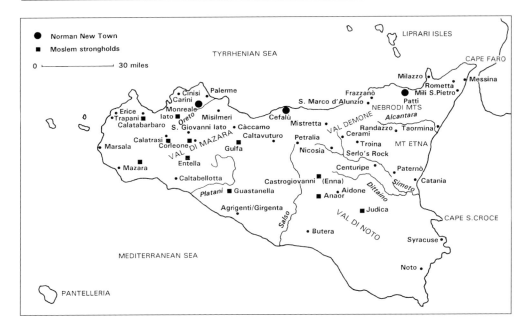

72   *Map of Norman Sicily*

In the summer of 1063 Ibn Hawwas received reinforcements from Africa. Nevertheless, despite adverse odds, the Norman forces were able to defeat the Moslems at the battle of Cerami, the most significant single battle of the entire Sicilian campaign. According to Malaterra, 'Loaded down with booty, the Normans now installed themselves in the tents of the Mahommedans, seizing their camels and all else they found there'. It is said that Roger sent four camels to Pope Alexander II from the spoils that the Normans collected from the Moslem camp, and in return received a papal banner. The Emir of Palermo was killed at the battle of Cerami leaving the Moslem capital in a vulnerable position. Added to this an envoy of Pisans approached Roger in Troina proposing a joint operation against Palermo. Roger's hesitation to take full advantage of the situation can only be explained in terms of his perennial lack of manpower, a predicament that precluded large-scale military operations unless his forces were reinforced by those of his brother, Robert. Thus with no hope of any immediate reinforcements from the mainland, Roger contented himself with plundering expeditions until Robert finally broke away from Apulia in 1064 and joined Roger in a campaign aimed at securing Palermo. However, Robert was soon obliged to return to his problems on the mainland, which were to take several more years to settle, and in the meantime Roger continued his raids in Sicily, accomplishing little of lasting significance. While on a plundering expedition in the vicinity of Palermo in 1068, Roger unexpectedly ran into a large African force of the Moslem army under the command of Ayub, the son of the Caliph Temin, and, despite the odds, the Normans won the ensuing battle. Amongst the spoils Roger discovered carrier pigeons which, according to Geoffrey Malaterra, he used to send word to Palermo of the

Moslem defeat. This battle appears to have been a turning point, weakening subsequent Moslem resistance in Sicily and prompting Ayub's return to Africa.

After Robert had re-established his hold on Calabria (1071) the brothers planned a new expedition against Palermo. Roger managed to regain control of Catania in eastern Sicily where Robert joined him, and there the two prepared a navy consisting of Calabrians and Greeks, ostensibly to be used for an expedition to Malta. Instead it sailed against Palermo and in August the Norman forces began a siege of the city by land and sea. A North African contingent came to the help of the beleaguered metropolis and succeeded in penetrating the blockade, but in the process suffered severe losses. The siege lasted for several months, but on 10 January 1072 the city surrendered and Robert, Duke of Apulia, made his formal entry into Palermo. He was followed by his brother Roger and by the Norman lords who had fought with him in the Sicilian campaign. They rode through the city to the ancient basilica of S. Maria, now hastily re-consecrated after 240 years' service as a mosque. Here the service of thanksgiving was performed according to the Greek rite by the old Archbishop of Palermo — who we are told 'although a timid Greek, had continued to follow the Christian religion as best he could' — and, according to Amatus, 'the very angels of heaven added their voices to those of the congregation' in celebration of the re-establishment of Christianity on the island.

At the time of the Norman Conquest, Palermo was a busy commercial metropolis boasting no less than 300 mosques — in the largest of which, formerly a Christian church, were said to be preserved the remains of Aristotle suspended in a casket from the roof — countless markets, exchanges, streets of craftsmen and artisans, and one of the first paper-mills in Europe. A probable product of this mill is the oldest dated European paper document, a deed dated 1102 signed by Roger. Parks and pleasure-gardens surrounded the city. Amatus writes enthusiastically of how, after the capture of Palermo, the Normans shared out 'the palaces and all that they found outside the city, and gave to the nobles the pleasure-gardens full of fruit and watercourses; while even the knights were royally provided for in what was veritably an earthly paradise' (**73**). From the outset the Normans practised a policy of coexistence with the Moslems that was to be an important characteristic of their rule in Sicily. The Moslem population was given assurances of the protection of life, religion and laws; despite the means by which they acquired power and the crusading complexion of the Sicilian campaign, the Normans in the south were, for the most part, tolerant of religious differences except, significantly, within the Christian church.

After the capture of Palermo Robert Guiscard never returned to Sicily; as a result, Roger's military options were severely limited. In place of extended campaigns the count had to rely on raids conducted from strategically placed fortresses, waiting for the right opportunity to force individual cities into submission (**74**). On the other hand, because the Moslem cities in the south half of the island acted independently of one another, and rarely together with the powers of North Africa, Roger did not face any concerted opposition. The Moslem retaliatory campaigns also tended to resemble raids more than set battles. In 1076 the Emir of Syracuse took advantage of one of Roger's trips to the mainland to launch an attack on Catania during which Roger's son-in-law, Hugo, was killed. Roger responded with a series of ferocious raids in the province of Noto and these destroyed so much agricultural land that they were held responsible for a serious famine

73   Mosaic showing exotic foliage and animals from the Royal Palace, Palermo

in Sicily. In 1077 Roger accepted the surrender of Trapani and Castranova and two years later Taormina fell after a siege. In April 1086 Roger besieged Agrigento; the city opened its gates in July and from there the Norman army moved on to Castrogiovanni (Enna) where Roger negotiated a surrender. The emir and his family agreed to convert to Christianity and were relocated, having been given territory in Calabria near Maletto. Roger was now in control of all of Sicily with the exception of Noto and Buterra. In 1091 Buterra and Noto, the last Moslem cities on the island, finally capitulated and the Norman conquest of Sicily was at last complete.

Once in complete control of the island Roger emulated William the Conqueror in England and set out to dismantle Sicily's Greek church and replace it with the Roman church. He oversaw the construction of new churches and appointed western bishops to key positions. These included Guerland of Savoy as bishop of Agrigento, Stephen of Rouen as bishop of Massara, Stephen of Provence as bishop of Syracuse and Angenius of Brittany as bishop of Catania. At the same time he began establishing western monasticism in the island by importing large numbers of Benedictine monks from the mainland. Roger jealously guarded his control of ecclesiastical affairs on the island to the point that in July 1098 he succeeded in securing for himself and his heirs the rights of Papal Legate to Sicily. The Greek church had been greatly weakened by the two centuries Sicily had been in Arab hands, but nevertheless there is little doubt that the imposition of

74(a)   The Norman Castle at Misilmeri. The Moslem fortress on this site was one of the last to fall before the capture of Palermo

the western church on the island would have been very unpopular with large sections of the Christian community. Many of these ecclesiastical changes were not the direct work of the Normans, but due to the arrival of large contingents of émigré mainlanders from Campagnia, Apulia, Liguria, Tuscany and even from north of the Alps. The insistence of Norman and Frankish conquerors on replacing the Orthodox with the Latin church throughout the eastern Mediterranean was a source of deep bitterness among the Byzantines. They often felt that they had more in common with the Moslems than with their fellow Christians, whose reforming activities were a source of conflict right up to the fall of Constantinople to the Turks in 1453.

The Norman army that had conquered Sicily was ethnically composite in complexion; its aristocracy was Norman, but its troops included a significant number of Italians. The Norman possessions in the island were partitioned between the two brothers; Guiscard retained the suzerainty of the island and half of Palermo, the rest fell to Roger who was invested as count of Sicily. He began the division of his possessions in Sicily and Italy into fiefs and distributed them amongst members of his family and his followers. Sicily, with its large Greek and Moslem population, thus became feudal.

The conquest of Sicily was accomplished in 30 years (1061–91) and was largely the work of a single individual, Count Roger, though at various stages he received vital help from his brother Robert Guiscard. The conquest might have been achieved more rapidly, but Roger was only able to call upon those forces that could be spared from the major

74(b)   Norman castle motte in Sicily

Norman commitments and confrontations elsewhere in Italy and the Mediterranean. With the death of his brother Robert Guiscard in 1085, Count Roger became increasingly powerful; he represented stability and power amidst the general anarchy that was congenital to the other Norman dominions of Italy. In 1090, just before the final capitulation of Sicily, Roger conquered the islands of Malta and Gozo which were still under Moslem control, although he left them under a framework of Moslem government. In return for his services in arbitration, Roger of Sicily also extorted from his nephew Roger — who had inherited Robert Guiscard's possessions — strongholds in Calabria as well as Guiscard's half of Palermo. There remained separate dukes in Apulia, Capua and Torento, but the dominant power was Roger, Count of Sicily, who was one of the most powerful rulers in Europe.

The Norman kings

Count Roger died on 22 June 1101 aged 70 years, in his mainland capital of Mileto. He was buried in the abbey of S.S. Trinita, which he had founded there, but which was completely destroyed by an earthquake in 1783. Although Roger had fathered numerous illegitimate children, he only had three legitimate sons. Geoffrey, the eldest, was a leper, and Simon and Roger, by his wife Adelaide, a north Italian aristocrat, were both minors. Following Roger's death in 1101 Adelaide, his widow, ruled Sicily as regent, mainly with the help of Greek and Arab ministers. On the death of Adelaide's eldest son Simon in September 1105, Count Roger's only surviving eligible male heir, Roger, succeeded him at the age of nine. Little is known of Roger II's childhood, though there is an undocumented tradition that he was baptised by St Bruno, founder of the Carthusian

Order. He spent his early years in Calabria and Messina, but in 1112, still only 16 years old, he was knighted in Palermo, in the old palace of the emirs, and subsequently he assumed responsibility for government. His father Duke Roger I and his other Hauteville uncles had been essentially Norman adventurers. In contrast, Roger's son was a Mediterranean man who, having been deprived of paternal influence from the age of five, had been brought up in a cosmopolitan, multi-lingual world of Greek and Moslem tutors, where state affairs were conducted in four languages. Roger was a ruler for whom diplomacy was more natural than violence and his contemporaries were soon to learn, sometimes to their cost, that he was not only a southerner but that he also had a strong oriental strain in his character. The court geographer whimsically observed that Roger 'accomplished more in his sleep than others did in their waking day'. Although Roger was a good western Christian and responsible for introducing northern European religious orders, notably the Cistercians, into southern Italy, he lived his personal life in an Ottoman fashion, with a harem (probably all Moslem) guarded by eunuchs. An advantage of his multiculturalism was that he enjoyed a more comfortable relationship with his eastern neighbours than his father and uncles, which provided the base for an ambitious expansionist policy.

Roger had also inherited characteristics from his Norman forebears including their energy and ambition. These, combined with a gift for imaginative statesmanship, enabled him to profit from the fecklessness of his cousins and to acquire, in return for military aid against a rebellious baronage, their mainland territories. By 1122 all Calabria was under his control and in 1127, when Duke William of Apulia died without issue, Roger laid claim to the duchy. There was considerable opposition; many Norman barons resented the domination of the Hautevilles, whom they looked upon as upstarts no better than themselves, and the Papacy, which had been in conflict with the Hautevilles on and off for almost a century, feared such a powerful state established on its southern frontier. But his opponents were no match for Roger's special technique of armed diplomacy and, in 1128, Pope Honorius II was obliged to recognise Roger as all-powerful Duke of Apulia, Calabria, and Sicily. Thus, these territories were united under a single political authority for the first time since the great Byzantine emperor Justinian had re-conquered Italy six centuries earlier.

By the age of 32 Duke Roger was one of the most powerful and influential princes in Europe. Only one thing more was necessary before he could weld his triple duchy into a single nation and deal with his fellow rulers on equal terms — a royal crown. Two years later he was to achieve this prize. In 1130 Pope Honorius' early death led to the usual dispute over the papal succession. Because of the energetic advocacy by St Bernard of Clairvaux, Innocent II soon had much of western Christendom supporting him. His rival, Anacletus II, turned to Roger for support, which was offered in return for a coronation and, unexpectedly and against the odds, Roger secured Anacletus' election. As a consequence Roger II was crowned the first king of Sicily in the cathedral at Palermo on Christmas Day 1130 (**colour plate 29**). In the words of the Abbot of Telese, who was present, 'It was as if the whole city was being crowned. Such was the scale of the celebration in this, the most cosmopolitan of European cities'. Roger had essentially created and was monarch of what became known as the kingdom of 'the Two Sicilies'.

Pope Anacletus died in 1138 and in the following year, after the defeat of an army under his successor Pope Innocent at Gallucio on the River Garagliano, the Pope was taken captive. Subsequently Roger forced Innocent to confirm his rule in the Kingdom of Sicily, with the overlordship of all Italy south of the River Garigliano. After this he was quickly able to pacify his mainland possessions where his vassals, aided by the German emperor Lothair II, had kept up a state of almost permanent insurrection.

Under King Roger in Sicily the new kingdom grew increasingly prosperous and powerful. Roger was an intellectual who took government seriously and, although he had little love for the Byzantine empire which maintained its claim to its former mainland Italian territories, his upbringing inclined him toward the Byzantine concept of monarchy; an absolutism in which the sovereign, as God's viceroy, lived remote and elevated from his subjects in a manner that reflected his intermediate position between earth and heaven. It is no coincidence that in one of the only two authentic portraits of Roger, the mosaic in the Church of the Martorana at Palermo, he is depicted in the robes of a Byzantine emperor being crowned by Christ (**75**). Indeed, there is no doubt that Roger believed that he was operating within the Byzantine tradition and that the Sicilian Normans maintained serious ambitions towards Constantinople and the ailing Byzantine empire.

Roger's government

Roger was able to build on the administrative foundations his father had developed, and created a civil service based on Norman, Greek, and Arabic models that was unparalleled in Europe (**76**). The government, centralised in Palermo, was divided between the *Dohana de Secretis* (finance) and the *Dohana Baronorum* (local administration) which was in the hands of the justices of the peace, and the men of the chamber were often Greek or Arab as well as Latin. The older Norman nobility were increasingly remote from central government, but this to some extent was their own choice and the power they did retain was later demonstrated during revolts they initiated under Roger's successors, William I and William II.

Palermo, the capital of the Norman Sicilian kingdom, possessed flourishing crafts and industries with palaces, administrative offices and a mint. Throughout the Norman period the Sicilian treasury and mint remained staffed largely by Moslems under the control of Greek officials. Many Norman coins continued to bear Arabic inscriptions, and even Islamic ones — though sometimes a cross was added, or the Byzantine legend 'Christ conquers' (**77**). The Italian word for mint, *zecca,* which dates from this time, is a direct appropriation from Arabic. Arabs also formed the spearhead of his army, while the navy was predominantly Greek. Its commander, who was known by the Arabic title emir of emirs, from which the word 'admiral' derives, served also as head of the government and ranked second only to the king in the Norman Sicilian hierarchy.

Although the northern European Normans were essentially land soldiers, in the Mediterranean they rediscovered maritime military techniques from the Byzantines and the Arabs and they created a navy that was used with great effect against their enemies. It was on this navy that Norman Sicily's security and prosperity depended, and Roger used

75   *Christ crowning Roger, King of Sicily — mosaic from the Martorana church, Palermo. Roger is clothed in the robes of a Byzantine Emperor*

76   *Twelfth-century manuscript showing the cosmopolitan Sicilian court consisting of Moslems,
        Greeks, Latins and Normans*

it energetically and to effect. Under the greatest of its admirals, George of Antioch, it subdued much of what is now Tunisia to form a profitable, if short-lived, North African Norman empire; it captured Corfu; it harassed the Greek coast, abducting Theban silk workers to work in the court workshops at Palermo; and in 1149 it sailed up the Bosphorus in a surprise attack on the imperial palace in Constantinople. Significantly, Norman Sicily played no direct part in either the first or second crusade, as many of the Sicilian advisors, medics and scholars were Moslems, and religious toleration was an important element in the court.

Another, more personal reason for not participating in the second crusade was that Roger had cordially despised the Frankish rulers of Jerusalem ever since his mother's disastrous remarriage to King Baldwin I of Jerusalem 34 years earlier and was not disposed to help the Latins in the Levant. Baldwin of Bologne, formerly Count of Edessa, had been crowned King of Jerusalem on Christmas Day, 1100. His first two marriages had been less than successful, but in 1112 he heard that Countess Adelaide of Sicily had ceased to be regent with the coming age of her son, Roger, and was looking for a second husband. Baldwin saw an opportunity to enrich his poor kingdom. Adelaide was immensely wealthy and such an alliance would bring the support of the Sicilian navy, which was

77   *Kufic mosaic inscription, Palace Chapel, Palermo*

already a force to be reckoned with. Her acceptance was given on the condition that if the marriage was childless then the throne of Jerusalem would pass to Roger. Thus in 1113 the Countess Adelaide left Sicily for the east. After an eventful journey the Sicilian convoy landed at Acre. Albert of Aix, a historian of the first crusade, recorded the event:

> She had with her two triremes, each with 500 warriors, and seven ships carrying gold, silver, purple, and great quantities of precious stones and magnificent vestments, to say nothing of weapons, cuirasses, swords, helmets, shields blazing with gold, and all other accoutrements of war such as are employed by mighty princes for the service and defence of their ships. The vessel on which the great lady had elected to travel was ornamented with a mast gilded with the purest gold, which glinted from far in the sunlight; and the prow and the poop of this vessel, similarly covered with gold and silver and worked by skilful craftsmen, were wonderful to behold. And on one of the seven ships were the Saracen archers, most stalwart men clothed in resplendent garments of great price, all destined as gifts to the king — such men as had no superiors in their art in the whole land of Jerusalem . . . The King, informed of his illustrious lady's arrival, went down to the port with all the princes of his kingdom and the members of his court, magnificently and variously clothed; he was surrounded by all his royal pomp, followed by his horses and his mules covered with purple and gold, and accompanied by his musicians sounding trumpets and playing on all kinds of instruments to delight the ear. So the King received the Princess as she descended from the vessel. The open spaces were strewn with beautiful carpets of many colours, and the streets were swathed with purple in honour of the great lady, herself mistress of such abundance.

However, soon after the marriage, Baldwin had already spent most of Adelaide's dowry, meeting debts and paying barons, knights and soldiers. It also transpired that Baldwin had not formally divorced his second wife. Popular feeling in Jerusalem rose against Adelaide and, in 1117, the Queen, penniless and humiliated, was sent home to Sicily. She died the following year and was buried in the cathedral at Patti. Later another historian of the crusade, William of Tyre, reported that this treatment of his mother, together with the failure to honour the promise of the throne of Jerusalem, imbued Roger forever with a violent hatred of the Kingdom of Jerusalem and its people.

Roger II himself was married three times. He outlived his first wife Elvira, daughter of Alfonso VI of Castile, and his second, Sibyl of Burgundy. His third wife, Beatrice of Rethel, whom he married in his last year, bore him a daughter Constance after his death. Constance was to marry the future emperor Henry VI, eventually bringing Sicily under the control of the Hohenstaufens. Roger died aged 58, on 26 February 1154. The life of King Roger of Sicily ended as it had begun, in relative obscurity. The cause of his death is not known although Hugo Falcandus, perhaps the most perceptive of the chroniclers of Norman Sicily, ascribed the king's death to 'exhaustion from his immense labours, and the onset of a premature senility through his addiction to the pleasures of the flesh, which he pursued to a point beyond that which physical health requires'. Despite his wish to be buried in the cathedral he had built at Cefalu, where for nine years a great porphyry sarcophagus awaited him, the king was buried in the cathedral at Palermo as a result of his long-running dispute with the Archbishop of Palermo (**78**). He was interred in another, simpler porphyry tomb, which has been opened on a number of occasions to reveal Roger's body still dressed in the royal mantle and Dalmatic, on its head the tiara and pearl pendants, such as is represented in his mosaic portrait in the Martorana church (**79a** and **b**). On his sword ring were engraved the words 'The Apulian, Calabrian, Sicilian and African, all obey my will.'

William I (the Bad)

Roger II was succeeded by his son William I (1154–66) who earned the epithet 'William the Bad'. William had, in fact, been crowned co-ruler with Roger three years earlier in what seems to have been a pre-emptive move to secure the throne for him. He was reputedly much less energetic than his father and, according to his biographers, left the business of state to his ministers, notably an 'eminence grise' called Maio of Baia (Palace Party) (**80a** and **b**). During his reign the Byzantines reoccupied a number of Norman held towns in southern Italy, papal forces marched against him and there were revolts by his own vassals. In 1156 however, William was able to subdue the rebels and reoccupy the towns which the Byzantines had taken, and eventually Pope Hadrian IV confirmed him in his Sicilian and Italian dominions. But William's troubles continued and the country began to divide into rival factions, one led by Maio his chief minister, consisting of disaffected nobles, many of them descendants of the original Norman conquerors. The citizens of Palermo formed another faction. Eventually Maio was assassinated and William was able to restore order. However William's reign was not a happy one, and the disorder in Sicily had its counterpart in North Africa where, by 1160, William I lost the imperial outpost built up by his father and his admiral, George of Antioch.

78   *Interior, Cefalu cathedral*

79(a)   King Roger's porphrey tomb, Palermo cathedral

79(b)   The exterior of the east end of Palermo cathedral

According to contemporary chroniclers William was indolent and cruel, but it is debatable whether he deserved the title 'Bad' given to him by the historian Falcandus. He was inclined even more than his father to the pleasures of the semi-Moslem life of court and seraglio; like his father he loved to discuss literary and philosophical questions with scholarly Greeks and Moslems (**81**). Before his death in 1166 William I had appointed his queen, Margaret, regent of the kingdom, but her power was usurped by a Council of Ten which was established by rebellious nobles. A particularly important if somewhat Machiavellian character was an English cleric Walter of the Mill, appointed Archbishop of Palermo in 1169, who succeeded in depriving the Council of Ten of the power it had acquired and who returned to the administrative policies of Roger II. He took the reigns of the government in his hands and retained the confidence of William II when William reached his majority.

William II (the Good)

William II (1166–89), unlike his father, was reputedly popular in the realm and is remembered in history as 'William the Good' (**colour plate 30**). He was a minor of only 13 years at the time of his accession and his actual reign began in 1171. Against the advice of his ministers he sent expeditions across the Mediterranean against Moslem possessions, a policy which was primarily driven by religious motives but also aimed at establishing naval and commercial superiority in order to protect Sicilian trade with the Norman

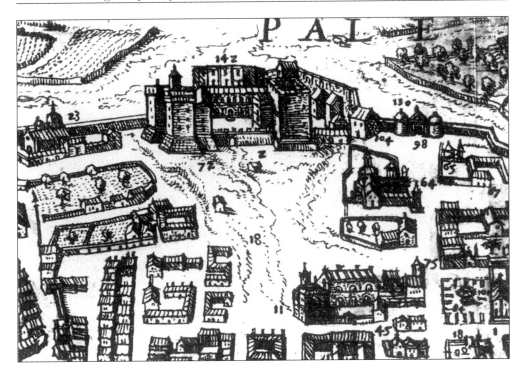

*80(a) Eighteenth-century plan showing location of Norman palace at the southern end of the walled
city of Palermo*

crusader state of Antioch. Its basic objectives were to keep communications open between
Europe and the Holy Land and to extend Norman protection to the Christian
communities of the Holy Land. William II was one of the first to assume the cross at the
beginning of the third crusade, though he did not personally participate and died in 1189.
William II never led his forces on the battlefield, but he was a shrewd politician and his
reign was relatively peaceful.

William was not a leader in the Norman military tradition, and rarely even appeared in
public. He had a reputation for loving 'luxury and comfort' and his constant exposure to
Arab culture led to his adopting many Arabic ways. He read and wrote Arabic and he kept
Moslem concubines and black Moslem slaves. A contemporary wrote 'He pays much
attention to his Moslem physicians and astrologers and takes great care of them'. Indeed,
during William's reign the whole city of Palermo was said to be 'imbued with the Islamic
spirit'. As if to emphasise the ease with which Norman Sicily could vacillate between
disparate cultures, in 1172 he had almost married the eastern emperor's daughter, but
eventually he settled on Joan, the daughter of Henry II of England and Eleanor of
Aquitaine and sister of Richard the Lionheart.

80(b)   Exterior view of Norman palace, Palermo

81   *Arab musician, Palace Chapel, Palermo*

82(a)   Norman fortress to the south of Palermo

The end of Norman Sicily

Following William's early death in 1189 the Norman kingdom in the south came to a rapid and untidy end. William II died childless and according to his wishes Constance, daughter of Roger II who was married to the German emperor Henry VI, should have succeeded to the throne of Sicily. But the Sicilian nobles were divided over the succession and in 1190 Tancred, a grandson of King Roger II, acceded the throne. There were several revolts against Tancred, including one by the Moslems of Sicily, which kept him occupied during the first year of his reign. After a massacre of the Moslems of Palermo, many of them took to the mountains of the interior and occupied some of the strong inland fortresses which they had held against the invading Normans more than a century earlier (**82a**). Moslem serfs who escaped from their Norman overlords joined them, but this revolt and its suppression were the beginning of the end of the Moslem presence in Sicily.

   The Third Crusade arrived at the doorstep of Sicily and Richard the Lionheart occupied Messina, but Tancred negotiated and came to terms with him (**colour plate 28**). The Holy Roman Emperor Henry VI was in the meantime planning to occupy Sicily, claiming the inheritance of his wife Constance. He concluded treaties with Genoa and Pisa in order to neutralise them, and in 1191 he laid siege to Naples and Salerno. The emperor had to return to Germany, however, because of an epidemic that had broken out in his army, and the empress was captured by the Normans at Salerno.

Tancred, the last Norman king of Sicily, died in 1194. William III, a minor, succeeded his father Tancred with his mother Sibylla acting as regent. Henry VI marched south again in 1194, concluded a treaty with the Lombard towns in mainland Italy, obtained the help of the fleets of Pisa and Genoa, and quickly and easily conquered the kingdom of Sicily, thus ending the extraordinary Norman chapter in the history of the island and of southern Italy. Norman rule in Sicily was replaced by that of the German Hohenstaufen dynasty with the crowning of the Holy Roman Emperor Henry VI as king of Sicily in Palermo cathedral on Christmas Day 1194. Frederick II was a semi-Norman successor, but Norman influence was no longer direct and Sicily ceased to be an independent kingdom, forming no more than a secondary element in the vast Frederician Holy Roman Empire. To many it was an ignominious end to the brightest star in the Norman firmament.

The wealth of Norman Sicily

Under the Roman Empire Sicily had been one of the granaries of Rome; its fertility and climate contributed to make it one of the most agriculturally productive areas in the Mediterranean, a characteristic which must have been particularly attractive to North African Moslems who had conquered the island in the ninth century. Indeed, Sicilian grain was exported in large quantities to North Africa during the period of Norman rule. Apart from the cultivation of wheat there are references in tenth-century writing to oranges and lemons, melons and almonds, while henna and indigo were grown for colouring. There are records of market gardens around Palermo and of machines used for irrigation. Arab geographer Al Edrisi wrote of dozens of places where fruit trees abounded. Also, Sicilian forests still played an important economic role both for fuel and building. Sicilian timber was used by Pope Innocent II to repair the roof of St John Lateran, and was also indispensable for the royal fleet. Additionally new planned timber centres were created by the Normans at Monreale, Patti and Cefalu (**82b**).

No other king in Europe had such large revenues as Roger, and his income from Palermo alone reputedly exceeded what his Norman cousins collected from all of England. Royal authority was usually strong enough to insist that taxes were paid, though some of his methods would have been impracticable elsewhere. There was, for instance, substantial revenue from numerous public baths, a survival from the Arab past which was unknown elsewhere in feudal Europe. The king engaged in commerce in his own right and his income from agriculture must have been considerable. He also retained the profits of justice.

Roger was able to tap the potential sources of wealth in a way that no subsequent ruler could quite emulate. An abundant currency was supported by African gold, and the ducat now made its first appearance in history. A merchant marine fleet grew up on royal subsidies, while the navy kept command of the seas and levied a tithe on ships passing through the central Mediterranean. Cotton growing seems to have diminished, perhaps because of the migration of Arab farmers and their replacement by north Italians, but the silk industry received an impetus from skilled immigrant Greek labour and the requirements of court ceremonial. A fine silk mantle still exists at Vienna with an inscription embroidered in Arabic to say that it was woven in the royal factory at Palermo

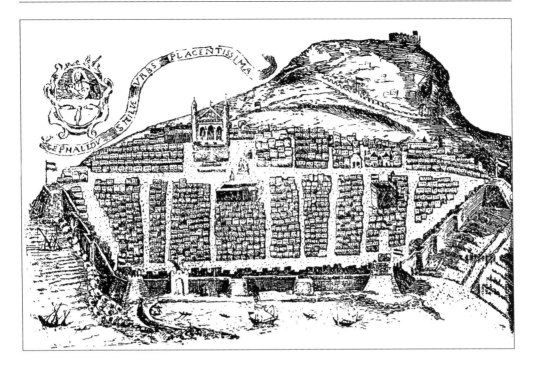

82(b)   Ancient plan of Cefalu showing the grid layout of the town in the twelfth century

in 1133 for Roger: this workshop was in the palace itself and contained goldsmiths and jewellers as well as silk workers (see **colour plate 29**). The mining of iron, salt and sulphur was carried on and coral fishing was already a major Sicilian industry. Fishing contributed a great deal to the royal revenue: the salted tunny fish of Sicily was, along with ships' biscuits made from Sicilian wheat, a regular food of sailors throughout the Mediterranean. There were special regulations that listed the points on the coast between which tunny could be fished when the shoals arrived in May, the number of boats and fishermen to be used and how much was due to the king. In contrast on the mainland, in Roger's struggle with the Pope and against rebellion in Apulia, villages were pillaged by both sides, crops were burned and vines and olives destroyed; conversely, visiting foreigners noted that no other prince had so peaceful and flourishing a realm as the island of Sicily.

The transformation of Sicily can be seen from its economic relations with its Mediterranean neighbours and the effect these relations had on the composition and commercial activities of Sicilian cities. For just as the island itself was Latinised so, too, were its trade routes. From the early twelfth century the Genoese, Pisans and Venetians were able to establish trading bases in Palermo and Messina, partly to service their longer trade routes to Syria and Africa and partly to gain access to the grain, cotton and other raw materials of the island. In the Genoese-Sicilian treaty of 1156, Christian shipping bound eastwards through Messina for the Levant was guaranteed safety; it was also guaranteed access to wheat, skins and raw cotton produced on the island. Gradually, the Norman Italians became the commercial force in the island and they also affected a gradual switch of Sicily's primary trading relations away from North Africa and the Moslem world towards northern Italy and the Christian west. The trade between Sicily and North Africa, initially in the hands of Moslems and Jews, was transferred into the hands of merchants of Latin descent, many of whom did not even live in Sicily. In the thirteenth century, Tuscan wine merchants furnished Tunis with alcohol and lines of communication linked Palermo to Champagne and Flanders. Even so, in the late twelfth century the majority of Palermo's merchants were still Moslem, while a century later they were mainly Latin. As early as 1160 it was recorded that a western merchant was providing loans to the Arabs in Sicily. Ibn Jubayr says of the Moslems of Palermo, 'In their own suburbs they live apart from the Christians, the markets are full of them and they are the merchants of the place.' Jubayr also says that the Moslems of Palermo were able to maintain mosques, but some such as the Friday mosque had been converted to the cathedral and San Giovanni delle Arimeti had a mosque at its core.

Not only were the great trading cities of Italy represented; Bologna, Piedmont and Liguria despatched significant numbers of settlers at the end of the eleventh century resulting in the colonisation of parts of central and eastern Sicily. There were particular links between the family of Roger II's mother Adelaide and Liguria that may help to explain the phenomenon. Some small towns still preserve place names and local dialects apparently of north-western Italian origin; Adones Nicosia and Novarra de Sicilia are examples of this phenomenon.

Al Edrisi in the 1150s called Palermo 'the greatest and finest metropolis in the world'. Palermo was, indeed, an opulent, busy town, far richer and larger than the Rome that the Normans a few years before had destroyed by fire. At the other end of the island Messina developed from a small fishing port to become an important centre of trade. Messina possessed one of the largest, deepest and most easily defended harbours in the Mediterranean and nearby there was abundant timber for ships. The narrow straits of Messina lay on the main route between Western Europe and the East, and after the capture of Jerusalem in 1099 the town flourished as an assembly point and a supply base for the provision of food and horses to the crusaders. Especially for French and Spanish ships, it was a half-way point to the Levant. A considerable Jewish community flourished in the port and a number of north Italian towns began establishing offices and wharves there.

Moslems, Jews, Greeks and Latins

Sicilian culture in the twelfth century had a distinctive oriental character and made its rulers an object of admiration and, it must be said, gave them more than a tinge of suspicion in the eyes both of northerners and of visitors from the east. The Moslem writer Ibn Jubayr who was in Palermo in 1184 commented on the large numbers of Moslems to be found in high government posts and at court, and the fact that they seemed quite free to follow their own faith.

Where Christians and Moslems mingled in places such as Toledo and Sicily there were scholars who could translate from Arabic to Greek and Latin, and from Greek to Latin.

Amongst the earliest of these in Sicily was Henry Aristippus, Archdeacon of Catania, who was responsible for translating Plato's *Phaedo* and *Meno* from the Greek sometime after 1150. Aristippus also translated the fourth book of the *Meteorologica* at about the same time. During the late twelfth century a number of other works in Greek were translated into Latin in Sicily, including writings by Ptolomy, Euclid and Proclus. The scholarly tradition continued into the thirteenth century after the end of Norman rule when, in addition to further translations from the Greek, works such as Rhazes' *Liber Continens,* a medical encyclopaedia, were translated from Arabic into Latin.

Such was the industry of the translating schools in Spain, Sicily and Constantinople that by the middle of the thirteenth century nearly all of the important works of Greek science were available in Latin translations. Some works were also translated into the vernacular languages, in particular into Italian, Castilian, French and later English. Of all these works the most influential were those of Aristotle who had provided the basis for the natural philosophy of the Greeks and of the Arabs, and whose work was now to perform the same function for western Christendom. The translations of his writings were chiefly responsible for the shift in educational interest that took place around 1200 towards philosophy and science. John of Salisbury (*c.*1115–80), the celebrated English scholar who travelled to Apulia to study Greek philosophy, had complained that the newly translated classical texts were, even in his time, being preferred to the poetry and history of his youth.

The Moslem Al Edrisi, a refugee prince from Morocco, was given the task of describing the produce and natural resources of each region of the world and of making a great silver map. The map was destroyed during the sacking of the royal palace by rioters in 1161, but his *Book of Roger* survives, a mixture of travellers' tales, of Arabic geography and of personal observations. Another major scholar was the Greek Neilos Droxpatrio who began his career at the imperial court at Constantinople, although he may have been of Sicilian ancestry. Roger II used his history of the five patriarchs in his constant battles with the papacy. The Greek scholar Eugenius translated Ptolemy's *Optics* from Arabic into Latin. These men worked at the court of King William I (1154–66), whilst others were drawn to the leading medical school of Europe at Salerno. Also, the Norman take-over resulted in the creation of a Romance language in Sicily, a young off-shoot of mainland Italian dialect.

Roger's court was also a centre of science. The king had a special interest in astronomy and astrology and his water clock was made by an Arab craftsman. According to an English monk who visited the Norman court, he employed a diver to investigate the straits of Messina and the treacherous currents which had created the legends of Sylla and Charlybdis. He took pains to regulate medical teaching and compelled doctors to undergo an examination by experts in the presence of a royal official.

In literature and scholarship the Arabs in Sicily produced nothing quite as impressive. There were some writings on science, medicine, jurisprudence and Koranic studies, and a list of about 1150 gives the names of some 100 poets from Sicilian-Arab families. Ibn Hamdis, the best known of these poets, was born in Syracuse *c.*1056 and later lived in Spain and Africa. His poems show nostalgia for the 'paradise of delights' and the voluptuous pleasures of Sicilian wine and gardens in flower. Little of this poetry has survived, neither do we know much about the French jongleurs that came to Roger's court with tales of Roland and the Paladins of Charlemagne. Norman French did not survive as a spoken or written language so well as in contemporary England, but French and Arab poetry together acted as a stimulus to the dramatic new vernacular Sicilian literature which began to emerge late in the twelfth century.

Perhaps a quarter of a million Moslems lived on the island at the time of the Norman Conquest making up about half the population, the rest being largely Greek with some Jews. The kingdom of Sicily has long been characterised as an island of tolerance, where Greek, Latin, Jew and Moslem are portrayed as living in harmony under Norman rule. Yet, to a large extent, this harmony only applied to the royal court, and repeated outbreaks of violence in Palermo in the mid-twelfth century demonstrated how fragile the peace was between communities even under the Norman kings. During the twelfth century Moslem farmers in the east of the island were displaced by Italians, in particular from the north of the peninsula. These colonists came to a relatively lightly populated island and, although many settled in towns, they were encouraged to cultivate unused or abandoned lands. One effect of the presence of these 'Lombardi' was the destruction of neighbouring peasant communities. In the 1160s the Lombardi, under their leader Roger Sclarvus, launched a series of pogroms against the Moslems, forcing them to flee westward to safe areas where the population was still predominantly Arab. It is true that there was also new Moslem settlement in Sicily, particularly during those times in the middle of the twelfth century when famines struck North Africa; many of these new migrants, however, were encouraged to return to their homeland. By 1200, the Moslems were already concentrated in the west of the island and on the higher ground to the south and east of Palermo. As their numbers declined so did the agricultural skills they had brought with them from Africa and on the Monreale estates, around 1200, and as a result specialist cultivation and crafts gave way to a concentration on wheat production.

The diminution in the Moslem population was also partly the result of voluntary conversion to Christianity. On the Monreale estates in western Sicily a new Christian generation of peasants emerged, some with names such as Phillippos, succeeding fathers with obviously Moslem names such as Ahmed or Mohammed. A similar conversion appears to have occurred amongst the Moslem élite of Palermo. Ibn Jubayr insists that William II made extensive use of Moslems at court, 'who all, or nearly all, concealing their faith, yet held firm to the Moslem divine law.' Conversely, as late as the mid-thirteenth century Latin landlords sometimes gave their children Arabic or Greek names if they lived among Greek or Arabic speakers.

The Arabic language survived in the most remote parts of the kingdom, particularly in the offshore territories of Malta and Pantelleria where there was an unusual degree of cultural autonomy. On the island of Pantelleria a Moslem population was able to survive relatively undisturbed. In Sicily itself the use of Arabic did continue, curiously enough in the hands of the Jews. Among Sicilian Jews Arabic remained an everyday language until their expulsion at the end of the fifteenth century. They gave their children Arabic as well as Hebrew names although they were not socially or economically isolated from their Christian neighbours at this stage. Until the late thirteenth century Jews lived together alongside Christians. As elsewhere in the medieval Jewish world, the Jews of Sicily harnessed a borrowed language for their own use. They Judaised it and yet the range of occupations among the Jews of Erice seems comparable to that found among Christians.

83(a)   Eugenius and other court members being led to prison by the Emperor Henry VI after the end of the Norman dynasty

There are certainly several Jewish physicians, as in other parts of Sicily. Gold- and silver-working, too, seem to have been a Jewish speciality. Jews functioned as carpenters, they owned vineyards and they made improvement loans in much the same way as their Christian neighbours. There is even some evidence to suggest a migration of North African Jewry to Sicily, encouraged in to re-introduce date and indigo cultivation as the Arabic population declined.

Unlike in Norman England slavery was a feature of Norman Sicily, but these were either domestic slaves, including concubines, or they were in transit awaiting sale in the slave markets of Palermo and elsewhere before re-export, possibly to the Moslem world. The Catalan slave handlers were middlemen who exploited the position of Sicily, close to the slave sources in North Africa.

In the later twelfth century the court as well as the country was being Latinised. After Roger II's reign there was an increasing emphasis on Latin culture as displayed by the rich neo-classicism of Hugo Falcandus, the historian, at the end of the century. The late twelfth century shows a significant expansion of Latin political influence at court (**83**). The Normans and the Italian baronage gained a place in the government of the kingdom, placing pressure on the Greek and Moslem remnants in the civil service. These Greeks and Moslems had been the major patrons of Greek or Arab culture and, as they

83(b)   Tancred, the last Norman king of Sicily, and Henry VI, contemporary manuscript

disappeared, the range of the court's cultural contacts contracted sharply. The same period saw the creation of close political and cultural bonds between the Sicilian and English courts, with each emphasising its Norman antecedents.

Art and architecture

The Norman rulers of Sicily that vied with the Byzantines for control of the Mediterranean modelled their representational arts largely on those of the great eastern power. Byzantine vestments were embroidered with Arabic lettering and worn by Norman-Sicilian potentates. Latin basilica type buildings were crowned with Greek cupulas and covered inside with mosaics, while Arab workmen devised decorations for Christian churches out of themes from Persian mythology. As the cultured Arab classes emigrated and as the Greeks were gradually swamped in the passage of time, it became clear that the different cultural traditions had mixed but never completely fused. To some extent, indeed, they depended on people who were not native to the island. By the 1150s signs were already visible that the religious tolerance which permitted this mixture of styles was wearing thin.

Norman-Arab art was an artificial creation of enlightened despotism, not a true inter-penetration which was viable on its own. Arab poets had not been influenced by Latin, but continued to embroider on traditional themes brought from Africa and Spain. Byzantine scholars similarly used forms and subjects imported unchanged from Constantinople. The lack of any true synthesis rendered this culture vulnerable and transient so that gradually the influence of France and Rome predominated in art as in religion and language. Roger introduced the Cistercians, Augustinians, Templars and Hospitallers, and with these came trans-Alpine architectural concepts. Northern barons and ecclesiastics were accustomed to building feudal castles as a symbol and guarantee of their power, and the Bishops of Girgenti were soon using stone for this purpose, taken from the old Greek temples. Feudalism thus became dominant in architecture, as it was in politics and social relationships.

Norman-Arab art and architecture did, however, exist as a vivid cultural phenomenon for most of the twelfth century. Woodwork and mosaic, coins and vestments, sculpture and lettering show how a heterogeneous mixture of styles could become almost a style of its own. The early Byzantine mosaics and frescoes of Eastern Europe and Asia Minor had been largely destroyed during the iconoclastic crisis and most of the later examples were destroyed in subsequent Ottoman invasions. Thus, those that survived in Sicily are amongst the finest examples of the art of twelfth-century Byzantium. While the best preserved early Byzantine mosaics can be seen in Ravenna, the best preserved mosaics of the late Byzantine period are to be found in Palermo (**84**).

St John of the Hermits, built by Roger in the 1130s with its five red cupulas, appears to be as much a mosque as a church (**85**). From the same period dates the church known as the Martorana, which the Emir George built for a convent of Greek nuns and endowed with a valuable library. This extraordinary church is embellished according to the classical system and is a prime example of this influence. In other twelfth-century churches in Sicily the Byzantine element appears alongside western European designs. Its grand plan was that of a Greek cross, and around the bottom of the dome in Arabic ran the words of a Greek Christian hymn. It also contains two of the finest Norman Sicilian figurative mosaics — one of King Roger and the other of George, prostrating himself before the Virgin Mary (see **71** and **75**).

Roger's finest architectural monument was the Palace Chapel in Palermo (1143 and later), which is a synthesis of a centralised middle Byzantine church and a basilica and therefore adopted a hybrid program of mosaics. According to Western custom the mosaics of the basilical parts depict narrative cycles; scenes from the Old Testament and from the lives of SS Peter and Paul (**85**). In the centralised part of the church most of the features belonging to the classical system are to be found; there is a bust of Christ the Pantokrator in the dome, surrounded by angels, but as a balance to the longitudinal axis of the church the Pantokrator also reappears in the apse. A western nave is completed with Arabic pointed arches on a Byzantine cupola, while the whole of the interior is lavishly covered by mosaic and coloured marble. The mosaics appear to have been designed by Greek craftsmen using Greek as well as Latin iconography. Opposite St Peter, the Bishop of Rome, was St James, Bishop of Jerusalem. Among the wood carvings of the honeycomb ceiling there are winged genii, veiled Houris, turbaned chess players, ladies on elephants and warriors on camels — some of them traceable to Indian and Persian legends.

84   *Christ Pantokrator, Palace Chapel, Palermo*

85   *The Abbey church of St John of the Hermits, Palermo. Although the church has eastern domes,
the attached cloisters are western European in design*

86   Mosaic of the building the Ark, Palace Chapel, Palermo

Two large basilicas are among the other high points of Sicilo-Byzantine architecture: the cathedral of Cefalu (*c.*1148) and the church of Monreale, the last of the great mosaic churches of Sicily (*c.*1180–90). Roger built the great cathedral of Cefalu as an Augustinian church attached to the new Latin bishopric that he founded during his quarrel with Pope Innocent. It was consecrated by Pope Anacletus and staffed with Frenchmen. Unlike many other Sicilian churches, this was a Romanesque basilica with a transept as found in the Latin West. The two towers flanking the façade show the influence of northern, or at least Apulian, architecture (**colour plates 31** and **32**).

Monreale consists of an immense complex of buildings, including a new Benedictine monastery and a royal palace sitting on an eminence overlooking the Conca d'Oro and Palermo, hence the name Monreale, originally *Mons Regalis* (the royal mountain). The abbot became bishop, and as early as 1183 it was raised to an archbishopric. The king invested his foundation with privileges and extensive estates so that Monreale was richer than the archbishopric of Palermo. In addition, he stipulated that the cathedral here should become the burial place for his dynasty. Despite the royal rivalry with the papacy, the papal bull of 1183 by which Pope Lucius II elevated Monreale to the status of an archbishopric states that William II 'in a short time, raised a temple to the Lord worthy of such great admiration that never had a similar work been carried out by any other king since ancient times'. William brought 100 Benedictine monks from the mainland to work

87   The ornate cloisters at Monreale

on the monastery. The monks landed in a royal trireme in March 1176. The king met the monks, accompanied them to their new home and handed them to Theobald, first abbot and bishop of Monreale. The Benedictines remained responsible for the religious functions of the cathedral right up until 1867 (**87**).

The cathedral is in the form of a basilica with three aisles in the shape of a cross, 335 ft long, 130 ft wide and 115 ft high. The west side is a twin towered façade typical of Norman architecture throughout Europe, and in front of the left tower, which remains unfinished, an atrium stood. However, whereas the west end of the cathedral is in the traditional western European style, the east end with its three apses is essentially Italian Romanesque with overlapping false arches and varied decorations made of chalk and black lava. The two bronze doors are also noteworthy; the west one was the work of Bonnano Pisano (1186) and is the largest bronze door of its age made up of 42 squares, each depicting a Biblical scene. Four reliefs make up its base incorporating animals symbolising man's foolishness. The smaller north door by Barazano of Trani is more or less contemporary but smaller, consisting of 28 panels depicting saints and evangelists.

Inside there is a nave with three aisles, which are separated by mainly ancient columns of unknown provenance with Corinthian capitals. The central aisle has a richly painted open roof truss, which was restored after a fire in 1811. Over the crossing an octagonal dome is thought to have been planned but never executed. The marble floor dates from the time of the original building. In front of the crossing pillars in the central aisle, underneath mosaic pictures of William II, stand the thrones of the king on the left and the

88(a)   The cloister arches at Monreale

*88(b) Detailed drawing of
column of cloister arch,
Monreale*

89   *La Ziza, a hunting lodge which lay in a park outside northern Palermo*

bishop on the right. In the right hand aisle of the sanctuary is the white porphyry sarcophagus of William I (1154–66) and the marble sarcophagus in which William II (1166–89) rests. On the left wall there is the urn with the heart of the canonised French king Louis IX, who died in Carthage in 1270 during a crusade to North Africa.

It is, however, the mosaics here that leave the greatest impression. They reflect the spirit of Byzantine culture and cover all the walls, no less than 6500 square metres, and were executed in just three years by artists from Constantinople together with local mosaicists. The central aisle is composed of Old Testament scenes and the side aisles depict the miracles of Jesus. The transept is devoted to the life and passion of Jesus, the resurrection and the apostles, Paul and Peter. The choir as usual is dominated by the image of Christ the Pantokrator, the ruler of the world, who has his place above his mother, Mary. Of particular interest is the depiction of Thomas Becket which is to be found in the apse. Thomas, a Norman, was only martyred in 1170 and canonised in 1173; the mosaics were actually being set when news of his assassination reached Palermo from the Pope's summer residence at Anagni (where a representation of the murder appears on an enamel box in the sacristy), and this may have served as a model for the Monreale mosaic. It is somewhat difficult to square the logic of this representation as, given William's own ambiguous relations with the papacy, you might have expected him to have sided with his father-in-law Henry II in his own dispute with the Pope. However, Sicily had become a favourite destination for friends and relations of Becket when the Archbishop was in exile. Also surprisingly, Sicilian clergymen played an important role in the search for a wife for Henry II.

The other extraordinary survival at Monreale is the cloister, which is the most significant remnant of the former Benedictine abbey. The 26 arches on each of the four sides open onto the garden characteristic of Norman Sicilian buildings (**83**). They are supported by double columns with double capitals. The columns are either smooth or encrusted with coloured stones, no pair of columns being like another. In the corners we find four smaller columns with relief work. In the south-east corner there is a chapel with a fountain with ornamental columns. In the centre a Moorish pillar with a zigzag pattern and sculptured decoration at the top of which the water runs out. The capitals are equally imaginative showing plants, animals, human beings, acrobats, archers, griffins and other fantastic creatures as well as Biblical themes — in other words the whole repertoire of imagery to be found in Norman architecture in western Europe. On the west side one of the capitals shows William II offering the model of the church to Mary. There is some dispute about the architectural derivation of the work here; some scholars claim it shows French provincial influence, others suggest a link with Campania, a third school supports the view that, although it clearly borrows from elsewhere in the west, it is pure Sicilian Norman. To the left of the cathedral stands the town hall which incorporates the surviving part of the royal summer palace.

The Norman kings created a luxurious pleasance in the shape of an extensive park outside the western walls. This royal park was embellished with fountains, ponds and buildings of various kinds, such as the Ziza, the Cuba and the Cubula (**89**). Roger's Park is described as follows by a contemporary chronicler, Archbishop Romuald of Salerno:

> And on certain hills and forests around Palermo he likewise enclosed with walls, and there he made the Parco — a pleasant and delightful spot, shaded with various trees and abounding with deer and goats and wild boar. And here also he raised a palace, to which the water was led in underground pipes from springs whence it flowed ever sweet and clear. And thus the King, being a wise and prudent man, took his pleasure from these places according to the season. In the winter and in Lent he would reside at the Favara, by reason of the great quantity of fish that were to be had there; while in the heat of the summer he would find solace at the Parco where, with a little hunting, he would relieve his mind from the cares and worries of state (**90**).

It has been suggested that this park with its artificial pools and fountains was the inspiration for Rosamund's Bower created by Henry II near to the royal palace at Woodstock, possibly the earliest example of aesthetic landscaping in England (see **50**).

The Norman cultural achievement

How then shall we judge the Norman impact upon southern Italy and Sicily, which was scarcely less than that upon England? At least they brought unity, and the kingdom established by Roger II in 1130 lasted effectively until the nineteenth century. In other ways, too, the Norman enterprise in the south changed the course of history. They contributed by their exploits to the fateful schism then developing between the Latin and

90   *Mosaic hunting scene, Palace Chapel, Palermo*

Greek churches and between east and west. At the same point they were responsible for bringing southern Italy and Sicily firmly into the world of Latin Christendom. In doing so they achieved the first substantial gain by the west from Islam which had once threatened to overwhelm it. Furthermore, while the Normans bore a papal banner before them in both Sicily and England, in Italy, as the allies of Rome, they contributed directly to the triumph of the re-founded papacy and all that followed from it, even to the virtual destruction of the powers of the medieval German empire in the thirteenth century. But perhaps their most extraordinary creation was the brilliant culture and civilisation of the twelfth-century kingdom; the amalgamation by Norman power of the wealth and eclecticism of four worlds, Latin, Jewish, Greek and Moslem. Scholars differ over the use of the term 'Norman' to describe the resulting mixture but, irrespective of nomenclature, there are few who would argue that the result was one of the most extraordinary and brilliant artistic achievements in the whole of medieval Christendom.

Further reading

General

Allen Brown, R. *Anglo-Norman Studies: Proceedings of the Battle Conference on Anglo-Norman Studies*, 1–4 (1979–82), continued from 1983 as *Anglo-Norman Studies*, (Woodbridge, 1979–)

Cassady, R.F., *The Norman Achievement* (London: 1986)

Davis, R.H.C., *The Normans and their Myth* (London: 1968)

Davis, R.H.C., *A History of Medieval Europe* (2nd ed London: 1988)

Douglas, D.C., *The Norman Achievement* (London: 1969)

Holmes, G., (ed), *Oxford Illustrated History of Medieval Europe* (Oxford: 1988)

Le Patourel, J., *The Norman Empire* (Oxford: 1976)

Mathew, D., *Atlas of medieval Europe* (Oxford: 1983)

Reynolds, S., *Kingdoms and Communities in Western Europe 900–1300* (Oxford 1997)

Saul, N. (ed), *England in Europe 1066–1453* (London: 1994)

Szarmach, P.E., Tavormina, M.T., Rosenthal, J.T., *Medieval England: An Encyclopaedia* (New York and London: 1998)

1   Vikings, Norsemen and Normans

The Making of Normandy

Bates, D., *Normandy Before 1066* (London: 1982)

Graham-Campbell, J., *The Viking World* (2nd ed London: 1989)

James, E., *The Origins of France* (London: 1982)

King, P.D., *Charlemagne* (London: 1986)

Sawyer, P. (ed), *The Oxford Illustrated History of the Vikings* (Oxford: 1997)

2   Normandy in the first half of the eleventh century

Bates, D., *Normandy Before 1066* (London: 1982)

Duby, G., *France in the Middle Ages 987–1440* (Oxford: 1991)

Fawtier, R., *The Capetian Kings of France 987–1327* (London: 1960)

Bates, D. and Curry, A., *England and Normandy in the Middle Ages* (London: 1994)

Hallam, E.M., *Capetian France* (London: 1980)

Shopkow, L., *History and Community* (Washington: 1997)

3   The Conquest of England

Bates, D., *William the Conqueror* (London: 1989)

Bradbury, J., *The Battle of Hastings* (Strand: 1998)

Douglas, D.C., *William the Conqueror* (London: 1964)
Hicks, C. (ed), *England in the Eleventh Century* (Stanford: 1992)
Higham, N.J., *The Death of Anglo-Saxon England* (London: 1997)
Stenton, F.M., *Anglo-Saxon England* (3rd ed Oxford: 1971)
Walker, I.W., *Harold: The Last Anglo-Saxon King*, (Stroud: 1997)

4   England and Normandy in the twelfth century

Barlow, F, *William Rufus* (London: 1983)
Bradbury, J., *Stephen and Matilda: The Civil War of 1139–53* (Stroud: 1996)
Chibnall, M., *The Empress Matilda* (Oxford: 1991)
Douglas, D.C., *The Norman Fate, 1100–1154* (London: 1976)
King, C. (ed), *Medieval England* (London:1988)
Poole, A.L., *Domesday Book to Magna Carta 1087–1216* (2nd ed Oxford: 1955)
Powicke, F.M., *The Loss of Normandy* (2nd ed Manchester: 1961)

5   The fabric of Anglo-Norman England

Chibnall, M., *The World of Orderic Vitalis* (Woodbridge: 1983)
Barlow, F., *The Norman Conquest and Beyond* (London 1983)
Holt, J.C., *Colonial England, 1066–1215* (London: 1997)

6   Aspects of Anglo-Norman society

Chibnall, M., *Anglo-Norman England, 1066–1166* (Oxford: 1986)
Green, J.A., *The Aristocracy of Norman England* (Cambridge: 1997)
Williams, A., *The English and the Norman Conquest* (Woodbridge: 1995)

7   The Normans in southern Europe

Bonet, Paul Neveux, F. (ed), *Les Normands en Méditerranée* (Caen: 1994)
Kennedy, H., *Crusader Castles* (Cambridge: 1994)
Norwich, J.J., *Byzantine* (London: 1997)
Norwich, J.J., *The Normans in Sicily* (London: 1992)
Phillips, J. (ed), *The First Crusade* (Manchester: 1997)
Riley-Smith, J., *The First Crusaders 1095–1131* (Cambridge: 1997)
Tyerman, G., *England and the Crusades 1095–1588* (Chicago and London: 1988)
Wolf, K.B., *Making History* (Philadelphia: 1995)

8   The Norman Kingdom of Sicily

Jamison, E., *Admiral Eugenius of Sicily* (Oxford: 1957)
Mathew, D., *The Norman Kingdom of Sicily* (Cambridge: 1992)
Tronzo, W., *The Cultures of His Kingdom* (Princeton: 1997)

Index